THE MAKING OF A
LEGIONNAIRE

Peter Macdonald

GUILD PUBLISHING

LONDON · NEW YORK · SYDNEY · TORONTO

THE MAKING OF A
LEGIONNAIRE

Peter Macdonald

This edition published 1990 by Guild Publishing
by arrangement with Sidgwick & Jackson Limited

CN 4737

Printed in Great Britain by
Butler and Tanner, Frome, Somerset, for
Sidgwick & Jackson Limited
1 Tavistock Chambers, Bloomsbury Way
London WC1A 2SG

Editorial & Design: Brown Packaging Ltd.,
255/257 Liverpool Rd., London N1 1LX

Editors: Peter Connor & Peter Darman
Design: Allister Cordice

I would like to thank the many serving and former
members of the *Légion Etrangère* who offered their help
in the researching of this book. They include: Jim
Wordon, Steve Mackay, Harris and the British contingent of 2 REP; Hedges and the English-speaking *sous-
offs* of 1 RE; Mike Nesbit and Jan Soholt. Also
Commandant Cockburn and Lt. Col. Mariotti of 4 RE
and Major Aubrey de Maraumont of 1 RE. I would also
like to thank the staff of the Legion magazine *Képi
Blanc* , the commander of SIHLE, Lt. Col. Terrasson
and Lt. Col. Le Roy and his staff for all their assistance.

My special thanks to the *sous-officiers* and legionnaires
of 2e section, 1 Cie, 4 RE, especially its commander,
Adjutant Edlinger, for introducing me to some of the
rigours of Legion basic training.

Finally, my thanks to Major H. Roos, *Président des Sous-
Officiers de la Légion Etrangère*, without whose help this
book would have lacked much essential detail.

**Front cover: A paratrooper of 2 REP wearing white *képi*, red
epaulettes and campaign ribbons.**
**Back cover and frontispiece: Legionnaires on patrol in the
deserts of Chad and the Horn of Africa.**

CONTENTS

PREFACE

"The doors of the Legion are open. We have nothing to hide. Nothing except, perhaps, the past lives of our legionnaires."
Legion Commandant General, 1990
The Legion still maintains its traditional policy of offering anonymity to those who volunteer for service within its ranks.

"The Foreign Legion is an integral part of France's Armed Forces."
Current Legion recruiting brochure.

"The French may believe that the Legion is part of the French Army, but in reality it is very different. It is also the best part."
English sergeant in the Legion, 1990.

The modern *Légion Etrangère* is a far cry from the Legion of old. Political activists, debtors, criminals and other 'undesirables' no longer flock to join its ranks as a means of escaping the law, their families, or other responsibilities. Such men are now weeded out by the Legion's stringent selection procedures.

Today's Legion is a Corps of professional soldiers, manned by individuals who take pride in what they do, and are prepared to undertake difficult and hazardous tasks in a world, which for many, has become far too staid and too civilised.

As in the past the Legion affords the chance to escape the monotony of dreary and dull lives, where one day is very much the same as the next. Above all, it offers a chance of adventure, a chance of seeing active service in a world where so many armies suffer from inactivity and boredom.

For those who wish for a life with an air of uncertainty and the risk of danger the Legion remains, its doors always open for the right man, regardless of his country of origin.

The spirit of the Legion means that no matter how tough the conditions or uneven the odds, the legionnaire will keep on to the end.

THE SPIRIT OF THE LEGION

What is it about the French Foreign Legion that draws men from all over the world to give up five years of their lives to serve in the toughest of modern fighting forces? The mystique of the Legion is based on more than 150 years of combat history, in which both individual and collective acts of heroism have combined to forge that unique spirit of brotherhood that defines the *Légion Etrangère*.

It is 11 o'clock on 27 April 1990. The weather is fine, the sky cloudless and the setting pleasant. The sun shines off the gloss-black painted railings surrounding a small park in the centre of a city. A group of men have gathered before the bronzed statue of a mounted soldier set to one side of the square. They have lined up, standing to attention, looking ahead. They are respectably dressed in suits, or jackets and ties. Their trousers are pressed and on their breasts they wear medals, one, two or more rows in some cases, others just a pair or a single decoration. They each wear a smart, close-fitting green beret, slanted to the left rather than the right of the British tradition.

The Legion draws its recruits from all four corners of the world, judging each man on his individual merits alone.

9

The unusual ceremony proceeds, and one by one three men are called forward to receive their decorations. The first to step forward is a Norwegian; the officer, and the medal with which he is being presented, are French. Another officer, also wearing a smart, summer service dress but this time belonging to the Norwegian rather than French Army, delivers the second set of decorations to the next two men. The men are of Spanish origin but the medals are in recognition of active service seen at Narvik in 1940. They return to the ranks to be addressed by an Englishman, in French:

'On 29 April 1863, Colonel Jeanningros asked

The Legion looks after its own, caring for those who have grown old or been injured in its ranks. This former legionnaire is attending the Legion's celebrations of Camerone Day.

Music and singing play an important part in the life of the Legion, whether as marching and working songs or, as here, the more ceremonial music of the regimental band.

Capitaine Danjou to organise a company as escort to a major convoy leaving Vera Cruz for Puebla. It was the 3rd Company's duty tour but, noting that all its officers were sick, Danjou proposed that he should command it. To assist him in this task, he took the standard bearer, Sous-lieutenant Maudet, and their paymaster, Sous-lieutenant Vilain.

'The column left at one o'clock in the morning on 30 April, intending initially to reach Palo Verde. Meanwhile the Mexicans, having learned of the passage of the convoy, organised a force of 800 cavalry and three infantry battalions — about 2000 all told — to attack it.

'At about 0500 hours Danjou's company stopped for a brief rest and, having posted sentries, set about making the morning coffee, which was well underway when the sentries announced approaching cavalry. In seconds the coffee was thrown away, the mules were re-loaded and the company was moving towards the outskirts of the village of Camerone — whence rang out the first shot of the battle, fired by a nervous Mexican sentry. The first cavalry charge quickly followed and was just as quickly broken up and repulsed by well-controlled fire, and by the use of thick scrub into which Danjou had moved his force. In the hubbub the mules took fright, broke loose and disappeared with the rations, water and spare ammunition. The 65-strong company had about 60 rounds apiece. Danjou decided to stand and fight, and to engage the enemy, thus distracting their attention from the valuable convoy, and rapidly moved his force into a defensive position in the nearby hacienda, where they were to hold out for the next 10 hours.

'By nine o'clock the sun was already high — the

This portrait of the hero of Camerone, Capitaine Danjou, hangs in the Legion's museum at Quartier Viénot, Aubagne.

legionnaires had no water, no food. Colonel Millan, commanding the Mexicans, called on the legionnaires to surrender — they replied that they had ammunition and had no intention of surrendering. The legionnaires promised Danjou that come what may, they would fight to the bitter end. He was killed at about 11 o'clock. At this moment, three battalions of Mexican infantry arrived on the scene, and again the legionnaires were called on to surrender. They replied 'merde'. The situation worsened — the Mexicans had broken into various rooms in the hacienda and, having killed the legionnaire occupants, had set fire to the rooms. For the wounded — intense heat, dust, smoke and no water. The battle continued. Vilain was killed just before two o'clock and Maudet took command. But by five o'clock he had only 12 men left in a fit state to fight.

'Again Millan called on the legionnaires to surrender. They did not deign to reply, and a fresh attack was launched against them. Maudet was now alone with a

The wooden hand of Capitaine Danjou is the Legion's most revered relic. It is kept in a glass case in the museum and produced every year on Camerone Day, 30 April.

Caporal (Maine) and four legionnaires (Leonhard, Catteau, Wenzel and Constantin). Their cartouchières were empty — they fired their final salvo and leaving their shelter, charged the Mexicans with their bayonets. All fell before reaching them. Maudet received two bullets. Legionnaire Catteau, who had thrown himself in front of his officier to protect him, was hit 19 times. They were the last.

'Here stood fewer than sixty men against an entire army'

It was 6pm and the battle was over. Maine, Wenzel and Constantin, though wounded, were still standing. Of the 65-strong company, two officers and 22 legionnaires were dead, one officer and eight men mortally wounded, and 19 to soon die of their wounds in captivity; 12 others, all wounded, were captured.

'When Maine, Wenzel and Constantin were called on to surrender, they said that they would not do so unless they were allowed to keep their arms, and to tend to their wounded; Colonel Millan replied; 'One can refuse nothing to men like you.'

'The Mexicans lost more than 500 men. The Emperor

Napoleon III had the title 'Camerone 1863' inscribed on the banners of the Premier Regiment; and in 1892, on the site of the battle, a monument was raised on which is inscribed:

ILS FURENT ICI MOINS DE SOIXANTE
OPPOSES A TOUTE UNE ARMEE
SA MASSE LES ECRASA
LA VIE PLUTOT QUE LE COURAGE
ABANDONNA CES SOLDATS FRANCAIS
LE 30 AVRIL 1863

(Here stood fewer than sixty men against an entire army. Its weight overwhelmed them. Life, sooner than courage, forsook these soldiers of France. 30 April 1863.)'

The English colonel completed his address and the ex-

This model 19th-century legionnaire is displayed in the museum at Aubagne. Like present-day legionnaires, he is well-equipped and protected from the elements.

legionnaires stood motionless before the statue of the French World War One commander, Marshal Foche. A red double-decker London bus swept by behind them as a Guards bugler played the last post. In the silence that followed, these former *soldats francais* reflected on the Legion's past glories; the battles of Camerone, Dien Bien Phu, Bir Hakeim, and countless others.

It's the intense camaraderie that makes the Legion so different to other units

For these silent men represented three generations of legionnaires. Some had fought against the Germans during World War Two, others against the Viet Minh in French Indochina, still others against the *fellagha* in Algeria. All had their memories, both bitter and sweet, but it was the good ones, the shared experiences and intense camaraderie of their life in the Legion, that had brought them together on this day.

The Legion is justifiably proud of its past achievements

Right: This tattoed legionnaire, pictured at the Legion's home of Sidi-bel-Abbès in Algeria, wears the faded khaki *képi* as opposed to the modern, white, *képi blanc*.

and puts great emphasis on its history and traditions, about which all new recruits are instructed immediately on joining. But it is the intense camaraderie between individual legionnaires, the special esprit de corps felt by all legionnaires both past and present, that makes the Legion so different to other units.

Over the past decade France has attempted to integrate its *Légion Etrangère* into the mainstream of the French military system. This effort has been only marginally successful, mainly due to the fundamental differences which remain between the Legion and other French Army units. Very few regiments in the French

Led, as always, by their Pioneers, the Legion detachment take part in the Bastille Day parade in Paris, July 1939 – only months before the outbreak of World War Two.

Serving and former officers of the French Foreign Legion join together in a traditional Legion song in the course of the Christmas Eve celebrations.

Army are totally 'professional' in the sense that they are entirely comprised of full-time, volunteer soldiers. Most regiments are essentially a compromise, containing a small 'regular' cadre and a large conscript element; in general, around 75% of a regiment is made up of conscript soldiers.

In the 1960s, immediately following the war in Algeria, the Legion underwent an intensive period of reorganisation. It became smaller, more streamlined and, above all, more selective regarding the recruits it accepted. When France has needed soldiers quickly the Legion has been less discriminating concerning the type of recruit it enlists. A good example of this can be seen in the increased intake of German volunteers in the years following World War Two. At a time when France was becoming heavily involved in its war in Indochina it recruited extensively from the pool of former German soldiers. The French needed men for her armed forces, needed them badly at a time when the vast majority of the French population had very little interest in pursuing a military career, even if it was only temporary.

Not only were former Wehrmacht and Waffen SS troops welcomed during the mid to late-1940s, but young German civilians and displaced persons (DPs) from all over Europe were also accepted and almost immediately pitched into a war thousands of miles away. Those who survived Indochina formed the basis for the Legion's order of battle against Algerian nationalists, a campaign which began as the war in south-east Asia ended. This sudden influx of German, Austrian and Eastern European nationals certainly influenced the Legion but did not change its basic character. The French Foreign Legion remained what it always had been, a French military formation largely manned of foreign volunteers — with the emphasis on the 'foreign' rather that the 'French'. The modern Legion has fewer Germans and more Frenchmen than it did 40 years ago. There are also, proportionally, more British legionnaires than there used to be, and more volunteers from Central and Eastern Europe.

Wherever recruits come from, they all share that desire for adventure that characterises the aspiring legionnaire. Since its formation the Legion has attracted men who want to see action, taste danger and hear shots fired in anger.

'A name that holds mystery and kindles the imagination — the Legion'

One current Legion recruiting brochure, printed in English and available from any good Gendarmerie, presents a stirring image of the Legion: 'a name that cracks like a rifleshot; a name that often appears in the press and in literature; a name that holds mystery and kindles the imagination: THE LEGION.'

The same brochure goes on to describe the Foreign Legion as an elite unit of international reputation with an impressive combat record including 'peacetime accomplishments', and asks the question 'what is it exactly?' It goes on to outline the Legion's history to date, its traditions, its uniform and its special anniversaries such as Camerone. The Legion's Code of Honour, its terms and conditions of service are listed and the brochure ends with a page of 'useful information', giving details of all the Legion's Information and Recruiting Offices in France.

The image that this brochure portrays is a fairly accurate, if romanticised, one. It provides an insight into why men join the Legion, as when it describes the 'average' legionnaire:

Parading the colours: while the FA-MAS assault rifles of these legionnaires are the very latest weapons, Legion ceremonies have changed little over the years.

'The Legionnaire is a volunteer. Most often, he has come to the Legion to escape his past. Generally, he has joined because of a personal or family crisis or an upheaval in his social or political life. Striking examples of this can be found in the mass enlistment of the Alsatians after 1871, of Spaniards in 1939, of Eastern Europeans after 1945.

'The legionnaire has bravely broken with his past and his family'

'For others, those who are unable to deal with the limitations of a middle-class life, the Legion represents a life of adventure. In the enlistment procedure, selection is very tough. Many candidates are turned down for medical reasons, or after a thorough study of their individual cases. The volunteer is seldom an angel but never a criminal. Once he has joined, under an assumed name if he so wishes, the legionnaire enjoys an unequalled protection for as long as he serves, because of the anonymity rule. Only he can decide when to break it.

'Coming from all corners of the world, with such dif-

A guard commander of 2 REP (2e Régiment Etranger de Parachutistes) watches his men form up for inspection. On his belt he wears a loaded 9mm pistol and FA-MAS bayonet.

ferent origins, languages and ideals, it would seem that they have nothing to share. But they have one thing in common: they refuse to be mediocre. Rejecting easy solutions, the legionnaire has bravely broken with his past and his family.

'Having lost his roots, he is ready to give all he has, even his life. This state of mind binds the legionnaires together and explains their unrivalled cohesion sealed with discipline, solidarity and respect for traditions.

'The legionnaire is first and foremost a man of action, extremely brave, who never loses trust in his leaders. This trust fosters attachment, and the ties between the legionnaire and his leaders include as much respect and admi-

Legion recruits at Castelnaudary bolt down a rapid mid-day meal during training. The rucksacks on their backs indicate the frenetic pace of the basic training course.

Former British legionnaires, spanning at least two generations, assemble with the French and Norwegian miltary attachés to celebrate Camerone Day in 1990.

ration as true and sincere affection. Alive he will follow them anywhere, dead he will never be abandoned.

'That's why one perceives the Legion as a large family. A man who has left behind his past, his social and family background, transfers to the Legion his need for an ideal, his affection equating the Legion with that of a homeland, to the point of sacrificing everything to it with a generosity which has astonished the world. That accounts for the motto on the front of the Legion's Museum: LEGIO PATRIA NOSTRA.'

The belief that a military formation can be a family to its members is a part of the ethos of many armed forces, but it is especially true of the Foreign Legion. More than any other French unit, the Legion has its own distinct corporate identity. It is small and close-knit, and everybody gets to know everybody else as they serve their time and advance up the command pyramid.

It is the legionnaires themselves who form the bulk of the Legion family, men from different countries and different walks of life who sign the five year contract and

enlist for service in the *Légion Ètrangère*. The majority of commissioned officers are drawn from the French Army, or rather are selected, from the top graduates of its officer training academy at St Cyr, to serve with the Foreign Legion. It is a high honour to be chosen and a successful attachment with the Legion can greatly enhance a junior officer's career prospects. If a young officer is especially good he may be called back at later stages of his military carreer to undertake a further tour with the Legion. In this way, a Legion regimental commander will have served with the Legion on three or four separate occasions before assuming command of his regiment.

Promotion to NCO is directly related to performance

Non-commissioned officers — sous-officiers — are entirely drawn from the ranks of the Legion itself. There are no attachments for French Army NCOs. Promotion to NCO is directly related to performance and an individual's physical and intellectual capabilities. Each man's previous experience, both within and prior to service with the Legion, together with his ability to command, is taken into account when a man is selected for promotion. In addition, there are examinations to be taken before a man can become first a *Caporal* and later a *Sergent* — and to become an NCO he must, of course, have demonstrateed the right personal qualities.

The bond between the legionnaires and their sous-officiers is the basis for the Legion's success. The men see far more of their NCOs than they do their officers; and since the sous-officiers have themselves risen from the ranks they have a natural fellow-feeling with the legionnaires they command — although it is a fellow-feeling that does not prevent them from maintaining a sometimes hard disciplinary regime.

'We believe in the spirit of the Legion rather than other qualities'

Whatever an individual's reason for joining the Legion, the terms of his contract are exactly the same as his peers' and his forebears' — five years, unconditional. The candidate must be between 17 and 40 years of age, physically fit and mentally capable. Any candidate under the age of 18 must bring his parents' written authority — that is the only prerequisite.

Just what the Legion is looking for in the volunteers was explained by Lieutenant-Colonel Mariotti, until recently second-in-command of the Legion's training depot at Castelnaudary: 'We don't pretend we want "Rambos", because we know that we have time within the five year contract to make an excellent soldier. We want to make a legionnaire into a man who feels confident within himself. In the first four months we will not make a "super-warrior", but that is not our aim. Instead we want to give them a sense of utility. Many are misfits, and do not realise that their abilities can be utilised. We believe in the spirit of the Legion rather than other qualities. To us the spirit of the Legion is devotion to comrades

The guard commander at 1 RE in Aubagne inspects the walking-out dress of legionnaires in transit before granting permission for them to leave the Quartier Viénot.

1ᴱᴿ ETRANGER

and total achievement of the mission.'

At the Legion's training regiment at Castelnaudary the recruits come together as a team for the first time since they joined up. During the first month the recruits get used to speaking and receiving orders issued in French. For many it is an entirely new language and they are likely to find it a struggle in the early stages. However, there will undoubtedly be a number of French-speaking recruits within the training platoon and these men, together with the instructors, have the duty of bringing the remainder up to a reasonable standard.

Cameraderie is essential to the way the Foreign Legion operates

By the time the volunteers leave Castelnaudary as trained legionnaires, they will have mastered a basic vocabulary of some 500 words. This knowledge gives them a basis from which to gain fluency in 'military' French at least. Whether or not they speak the language when they are off duty does not matter to the Legion; what concerns it is that the legionnaires fully understand what is required of them. By the time the recruit has completed his basic training, he has a very clear idea indeed of what is needed.

The essence of Legion training, apart from imparting the obvious military skills, is centred on instilling the volunteers with the esprit de corps which makes the Legion special. Cameraderie is essential to the way the Foreign Legion operates and is a quality that is fostered from Day One of training. To an outsider many of the ceremonies in which the legionnaires take part may seem outdated, belonging more to a monastic order rather than a modern fighting force. The ceremony of the *képi blanc*, when the recruits receive the traditional Legion headgear, is one such ceremony. Flaming torches illuminate the parade ground as the successful recruits march wearing their meticulously pressed dress uniforms. Speeches are made, Legion songs are sung and, when emotions have reached fever pitch, the men are allowed to don the white képis they have been holding behind their backs and for which they have worked so hard. The whole ritual is designed to foster the almost mystical feeling of being accepted into an exclusive brotherhood, the brotherhood of the

This corporal in 2 REP is armed with a highly-polished FA-MAS assault rifle. Chin straps, awards and medal ribbons are all part of the legionnaire's traditional parade dress.

Légion Etrangère.

On entering this new 'order' the volunteers receive the Legionnaire's Code of Honour, a seven-point oath:

'1. Legionnaire: you are a volunteer serving France faithfully and with honour.

2. Every Legionnaire is your brother-at-arms, irrespective of his nationality, race or creed. You will demonstrate this by an unwavering and straightforward solidarity which must always bind together members of the same family.

3. Respectful of the Legion's traditions you will honour your superiors. Discipline and camaraderie are your strength, courage and loyalty your virtues.

4. Proud of your status as a Legionnaire, you will always display this pride: by your turn-out, always impeccable; your behaviour, ever worthy, though modest; your living-quarters, always tidy.

5. As an elite soldier: you will train vigorously, you will maintain your weapon as if it were your most precious possession, you will keep your body in the peak of condition, always fit.

6. A mission once given to you becomes sacred to you, you will accomplish it in the end and at all cost.

7. In combat: you will act without relish of your task, or hatred; you will respect the vanquished enemy and will never abandon either your wounded or your dead, nor will you under any circumstances surrender your arms.'

The spirit of Camerone permeates the whole of the Legion

The Code encapsulates the spirit of the Legion and has been honoured in countless battles and campaigns worldwide. Individual legionnaires are not only superb soldiers but are also bound by the mystique and élan which surrounds this unique fighting force. The spirit of Camerone permeates the whole Legion and is purposely indoctrinated into recruits from day one. This spirit breeds bravery, loyalty to one's comrades and the Legion, and the ability to carry out orders in the face of overwhelming odds.

These are the virtues which the Legion hopes to inculcate in the thousands of adventurous spirits who arrive each year at its recruiting centres. For as General Négrier, a former commandant of the Legion, told his men: 'You Legionnaires are soldiers in order to die, and I am sending you where you can die.'

MAKING THE DREAM COME TRUE

The prospect of adventure and a new life in the ranks of the Legion draw thousands of hopefuls to recruiting centres in France every year. But the Legion will not take just anyone who walks in, and the process of joining up and initial selection at Legion HQ is one that can wreck the dreams of many a would-be legionnaire.

The French Lieutenant-Colonel, working for the Defence Attache's office in London, explained the problem France's *Légion Etrangère* causes him. It was not the Legion's fault exactly, he pointed out, the problem lay with the British. Every week he would get letters and telephone calls from anxious girl-friends, spouses or parents. They all had one thing in common. 'Where is Johnny or Jim or Harry', they would ask,'he said he was off to join the Legion, and we haven't heard from him since.'

An aspirant to the *képi blanc* arrives at a recruiting centre in France. Many volunteer for the Legion, but few are chosen.

Each week the Colonel passes on these enquiries to the Legion offices in Paris, including pertinent personal details and possibly a photograph of the adventurous individual. 'Has Monsieur A. Brown, an Englishman, joined the Legion in the past two months? His mother is anxious to trace him.'

The Legion offers escape for those who wish to disappear without trace

Often the reluctant correspondent will be traced and agree to allow his address to be passed to those enquiring after him. Occasionally, however, 'M. Brown' wants to make a clean break with his past and has taken advantage of the Legion's offer of anonymity. He is now Legionnaire 'Braun', and hails from Berlin rather than Basingstoke. The official reply, passed on to the relatives, is that 'there is no Englishman named A. Brown presently serving in the *Légion Etrangère* who has joined during the past two months.'

The French Foreign Legion still offers an avenue of escape for those men who wish to disappear without trace. Providing they have no criminal record, and meet the stringent selection criteria, they are welcomed. The price involves signing a five-year contract to serve as a professional soldier for France.

But just how does the foreign volunteer go about signing on with the French Foreign Legion? There are no advertisements on television or in the national newspapers. Occasionally the British newspapers print sensational first-hand accounts by deserters of life in the Legion, accounts which almost always emphasise the Legion's harsh training and the sometimes brutal discipline the author has suffered

Strangely enough, such articles actually aid recruitment, especially from Great Britain, and also have the

A Legion recruit undergoing his medical examination at Aubagne. The Legion has its own doctors attached from the French Army Medical Corps.

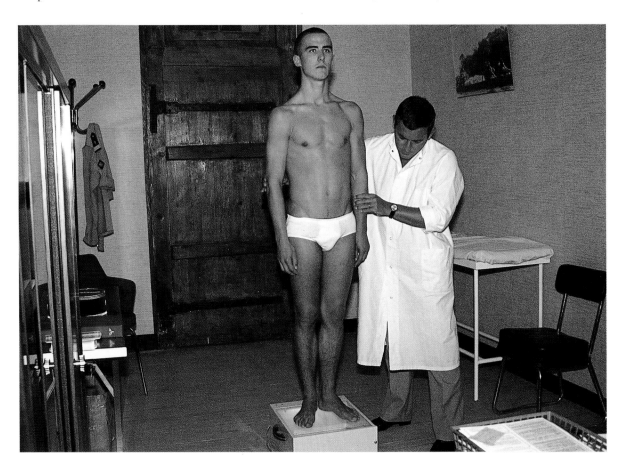

positive benefit for the *Légion Etrangère* of putting off the faint-hearted, thereby saving the Legion time, effort and money in training the uncommitted.

How does the foreign volunteer go about signing on with the Legion?

It has often been said, both within and outside the Legion, that British nationals are the most troublesome group. Today, there is little evidence to support this statement. One only has to look at the high concentration of 'Brits' in 2 REP, the second foreign legion parachute regiment and reputedly the toughest outfit within the Legion, to realise that the 'Brits' can make good legionnaires. As with any unit in any Army there are always the odd men out, men who for one reason or another are unable to settle down to the serious business of soldiering and are constantly in trouble.

One of the differences between men like this who happen to be British, and those of other nationalities, is that the 'Brits' who desert tend to be considerably more vocal about it. As a Legion major put it: 'Amongst themselves most Legion officers tend to say that the Germans make the best legionnaires. I disagree with this view. I feel that the best soldiers we have are the British. However, they are also the worst! If they settle down to life in the Legion they are good, especially in the field or on operations. If they cannot adjust to the Legion, if they cannot accept the peculiar, essentially French way of life — they cause the most trouble and are a very disrupting influence.'

The Legion plays the problem of desertion pretty close to its chest; no official figures are released and certainly there is no official breakdown as to incidence of desertion by nationality. However, speak to the legionnaires themselves and you will find that it is the 'Brit' element

The moment of truth: a Legion recruit signs on the dotted line. The five-year contract constitutes the longest enlistment period of any army in the western world.

that is most renowned for 'taking off' or, in the words of one legionnaire, 'escaping'.

For an Englishman, finding out how to join the *Légion Etrangère* can be a complicated business. Flicking through the telephone directory is out, unless you happen to have a copy for Paris. Getting in touch with the French military attaché in London is a better bet and, although he can do little to help officially (it is against the law to recruit for foreign armies within the United Kingdom), he may be able to put you in touch with a former legionnaire who will give you the run-down. His advice would probably be to go over to France and drop into the local Gendarmerie. There the prospective recruit will probably be met with a comment such as 'Not another crazy Englishman'. Should he earnestly wish to join the Legion such remarks will not be too off-putting, especially as they will be reiterated constantly while his application is being processed.

Each volunteer is then collected from the Gendarmerie by a local Legion representative, usually a junior NCO, before being transferred to a holding centre where he joins other would-be legionnaires. The actual initial joining sequence may well go as follows: a volunteer reports to a Gendarmerie at port of entry (say, Calais), is collected by a Legion NCO and driven to a holding centre (such as Lille) where the Legion maintain a presence in an Army barracks, known as a *citadel*. Initial interviews are conducted by SNCOs at this stage, and the weeding out process begins.

Not all legionnaires will live to see the expiry of their contract

During this period the volunteers mess on their own and are kept separate from French Army conscripts, although it is uncertain which group is protected by this segregation; legionnaires tend to assume the procedure is aimed at preventing new Legion recruits from picking up bad habits. If there is time, initial medical tests may be carried out before the volunteers are transferred to a metropolitan Legion 'outpost' such as Fort St Nogent outside Paris. In days gone by this would be the time that the volunteers received their regulation Legion cropped haircut, the '*boule à zéro*', followed by their first pay parade and uniform issue. Nowadays the haircut is inflicted by the barber at 1 REI, Aubagne, after the men have had an opportunity to understand the Legion and its ways slightly better. Fatigue duties such as washing details, the traditional pastime of all those in transit, occupy some of the recruits' time, although there is less of such 'bull' than there was in the past.

At regular and frequent intervals the volunteers are collected from their holding centres and transferred by train to the south of France. For instance, those at Fort St Nogent would leave from Paris's Gare de Lyon on a train to Marseilles' Gare St Charles and from there travel by district branch line to Aubagne's small railway station. The journey south from Paris can be a long and tedious one and those men volunteering for the Legion in Marseilles have a far less uncomfortable time than those who make the decision in Paris or Lille.

Coach transport is laid on to pick up the men and their

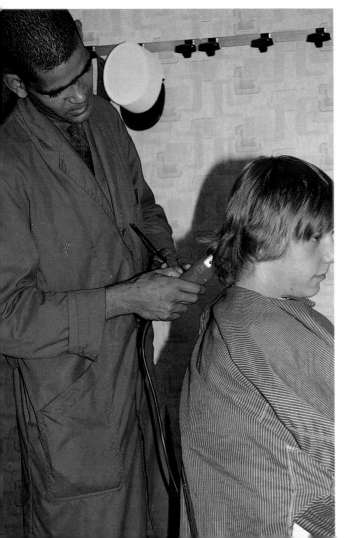

One of the rites of passage of the Legion recruit is the regulation haircut, the *boule à zéro*. This severe style sets the legionnaire apart from other members of France's Army.

escort from Aubagne station and transport them the three miles to Quartier Viénot, headquarters of the *Légion Etrangère* and home of 1 RE, the *1er Régiment Etranger*. This is the camp through which all volunteers pass on their way to basic training and to which all other legionnaires return in between postings and attachments. The barracks is well appointed and relatively modern.

Until the 1960s the Legion's headquarters had been in Algeria, at their traditional home of Sidi-bel-Abbès. Algeria had been the centre of the Legion since shortly after its formation, and had remained so for 150 years until 1965 when a sad and disillusioned army had 'returned' to France for the first time. Apart from the bitter-sweet memories the Legion brought with it the *Monument aux Morts*, the memorial to the Legion's dead, which now stands in the centre of Aubagne's Place d'Armées.

The monument, a globe resting on palm fronds, set on a square block with larger than life statues of legionnaires at each corner, is the first thing that the volunteers see after their transport passes through the front gate of the camp. The inscription *la Légion à ses morts* — the Legion to its dead — serves as a grim reminder that not all legionnaires will live to see the expiry of their contract. The volunteers still have their contracts to sign.

Their possessions are taken from them, bagged up and put into storage.

At Aubagne all prospective recruits are screened by the *Section Engagés Volontaires* and are interviewed by the Section OC. They have come from the main recruiting offices or PILE (*Poste Information de la Légion Etrangère*) at Paris, Marseilles and Strasbourg. There are normally two weekly intakes of EVs (*Engagés Volontaires*), as the Legion's recruits are known, and they will spend between two to three weeks (between 15 to 20 days) at Aubagne before moving on to Castelnaudary

A Pioneer stands before the *Monument aux Morts*, Aubagne. The monument was transported from Sidi-bel-Abbès in Algeria when the Legion withdrew in 1965.

near Toulouse, the home of 4 RE, *4e Régiment Etranger*, the Legion's training regiment.

At Quartier Viénot the EVs undergo their initial processing and are introduced to life in the Legion for the first time. Until now they have spent their time undergoing basic interviews, waiting to be collected from various locations around the country, and travelling southwards. It has been a slow, methodical process, but one designed to give the EVs time to consider the commitment they are soon to undertake — a five year contract to serve in the Legion. The volunteers will also have had a chance to get to know their comrades, the EVs with whom they will be training for the next four months.

On arrival all their possessions, with the exception of underwear and washing kit, are taken from them, bagged-up, and put into storage. They are given a basic kit issue comprising clean, used uniforms, boots, socks, track suits and running shoes. In fact they receive everything they need for the next two to three weeks. As for their personal belongings, they remain secured in storage until the men pass out of their basic military training.

A recent English recruit, with regulation haircut and wearing his new *tenue de combat*, gets to grips with French literature in the recruits' foyer at Aubagne.

They are then sold, and the proceeds donated to a charity such as the French Red Cross. If the volunteers are under the impression that the poor will end up wearing their expensive suits or designer jeans, they are mistaken. Prospective legionnaires would be well advised to leave all items of value at home before joining the Legion, or perhaps post it to the French Red Cross personally. As a Scandinavian corporal recalls:

'You can end up with a pile of rags brought in by a penniless African'

'I borrowed my brother's leather flying jacket, not realising I would "lose" it. Six months later I saw an American legionnaire wearing one strikingly similar. Perhaps he could have bought it from the Red Cross — but somehow I find that rather difficult to believe...'

The corporal, now serving with 6 REG *(6e Régiment Etranger de Génie)*, the Legion's Engineer Regiment and the new home of his brother's jacket, would have benefited from a talk with one of the supply sergeants at

Aubagne. This *sous-off* claims to have the largest collection of leather jackets in the Legion; he can only assume that either the one now worn by the American legionnaire did not fit, or that he already had one very similar.

All men are treated equal from the start, regardless of nationality or race

Another important aspect of the EVs' stay at Aubagne is that all men are treated equal from the start. Regardless of nationality or race they undergo the same induction process, receive the same kit issue, are given the same haircut and begin to learn the same language. The only difference is that the written and oral tests they take are in their own language, and that French speaking EVs are given the task of teaching their non-French-speaking colleagues the basics of the language they will be using for the next five years. The process of learning French is a gradual one but the *Légion Etrangère* seldom fails to instill the vocabulary required in the time allowed.

During their stay at the Central Depot Viénot Barracks, Aubagne, the EVs come under the command of the *Centre de Sélection et Incorporation* (CIS), the Legion's selection and recruitment centre. This unit is divided into three sections: *1er section*, responsible for selection; *2e section*, which runs EV *incorporation* or the basic induction process; and a third section, manned by experienced sous-officiers responsible for EV instruction, training and the administration of the other two sections. The *1er section* or 'green' section, runs the medical, intelligence, psychological and security checks.

'These guys would be feeding the interrogater a load of bullshit'

The first checks that the EVs undergo are medical, when a doctor assesses their general physical condition, gives them blood tests and arranges for x-rays. Once their physical fitness has been determined the men are handed over to the *Groupement d'Evaluation Psychotechnique* (GEP) for intelligence and psychological assessment.

Two levels (niveaux) of IQ test are carried out on the EVs by GEP — *générale* and *culturel* (NG and NC). These tests assess what the men have learned from life and what they have remembered from their school days. They are standard French tests, although the EVs take them in their own language, they include questions on general knowledge and mathematics, and are marked from 0-20. The Legion accepts those with grades of 6+, although those men who go on to attain *sous-officier* rank must have a minimum of 12 points. One point of interest is that the men are given these tests again after they have served in the Legion for three years. Regardless of whether their personal rating has risen or fallen, the higher figure is recorded on their personal documentation.

Once they have passed their IQ tests the EVs are handed over to the *Bureau des Statistiques de la Légion Etrangère*, which is normally referred to simply as BSLE, *Sécurité* or *Intelligence*. These terms have little to do with national security, which is more the area of agencies of the French Secret Intelligence Services such as the *Deuxième Bureau*. While BSLE does have close links

Recruits line up to get drinks at the evening meal. Food in the Legion is generally of a much higher standard than is found in other branches of the French Armed Forces.

A member of a recruit training company takes a wall on the assault course at Castelnaudary. Physical fitness is built up gradually over a four-month period.

with such organisations, and occasionally co-operates with them, the Legion generally looks after its own affairs. The men in the Legion's *Sécurité* office are experienced *sous-offs*, chosen primarily for their language abilities rather than other qualities. This occasionally leads to problems as one *sous-off*, temporarily attached to *Sécurité* as an interpreter, explains:

'Guys would come in, obviously with bad backgrounds, trouble at home, from broken families, skinheads with a history of violence and drugs. These guys would be feeding the interrogator a load of bullshit about their past, and the *sous-off* running the interrogation would be lapping it up. Others would come straight from school, with everything well documented, educational certificates, the lot. The interrogator, a Polish *Sergent-chef*, would be convinced that these men were lying. I'm a pretty good judge of character, and it was obvious they were telling the truth. "I think this one sucks cock" the Pole would say, or "he takes drugs". It was difficult because I would naturally sympathise with the guys

being interviewed. I'd tell them "he reckons you suck cock" which would surprise and upset them — but at least they were warned.'

Each volunteer attends at least two interviews. The first is a one-to-one with a *sous-off*, who asks the candidate about his past, makes notes on his background and assesses his character. The second interview is conducted by a panel. They double-check the EV on his background, cross-checking his answers with those given to his first interviewer, and attempt to ascertain the 'real' reason why the man wishes to join the Legion.

During the stay at Aubagne recruits are graded by colours; yellow after they have survived the first week, green for the second, and red for the third and final week. Once a volunteer passes the two interviews conducted by the men from BSLE he is accepted into *2e sec-*

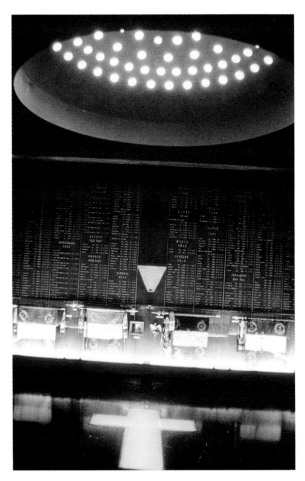

The museum at Quartier Viénot, Aubagne. It houses the Legion's relics, including the wooden hand of Capitaine Danjou and the battle honours of disbanded regiments.

ing facilities as the trained legionnaires, the EVs eat separately. Breakfast is followed by half an hour to an hour's cleaning of the barrack rooms, and the section parades outside the building at 0730 hours. The early morning parade is preceded by *corvée*, when the fatigue party cleans up the parade ground by marching slowly in line from one end to the other, shoulder to shoulder, picking

tion, the 'red' section. Here he undergoes *incorporation*, his induction into the Legion. The EV is given his haircut, the infamous *boule à zéro* which marks out the accepted volunteer, and begins his final week at Aubagne.

For the accepted EV the routine at Aubagne is slightly less severe than it used to be as daily life in the Legion has fallen more into line with the remainder of the French Army. Less than five years ago reveille was at 0430hours; today the EVs passing through Aubagne get to lie in an extra hour and reveille is not until 0530hours, when the men rise, shave, wash and parade. At 0600hours there is appel or roll call, when the section is checked to make sure all men are present. This is followed by breakfast in the main cookhouse. Although they use the same mess-

Members of the band practise before the *Monument aux Morts*, when it was in place at the Legion's former headquarters at Sidi-bel-Abbès in Algeria.

up scraps of paper and cigarette butts as they go. The parade is followed by medicals, interviews, intelligence tests, or, if the EV is not required, work details, physical training or lectures. Lunch, like breakfast, is taken early in the Legion and the EVs assemble at the cookhouse for their mid-day meal at 1100 hours. By 1200 hours the men return to their *section* and have free time until they have their next parade at 1330 hours.

At 1345 hours they are detailed for afternoon duties. What these are depends on which *section* they belong to, and how far they have got with their *incorporation*.

Dinner or the evening meal is served in the cookhouse from 1700 hours onwards but the EVs, unlike the trained legionnaires serving with 1 RE or those passing through Aubagne in transit, are working to a an extremely tight schedule. They eat at set times and as a group, watched over by their *chef de section* or his nominee. However, meals in France, even in the Legion, tend to be relatively unhurried affairs and the *engagés volontaires* have an hour to eat and digest their food down before returning to the CIS block.

Evenings for the *engagés volontaires* are not fraught

Evidence of the Legion's worldwide postings can take many forms. In this case a Legion unit in Djiboutii has taken a cheetah as a mascot.

with the same dangers as those that the trained legionnaire is likely to encounter. There are no wild, alcoholic binges in town, no brief encounters with the prostitutes who catch the late afternoon or early evening trains up from Marseilles. The EVs can expect a video on the virtues of Legion life or, if they are really lucky, an epic extolling the battlefield exploits of Rambo. This can be washed down with a soft drink in their own bar (definitely no alcohol) or a browse through the CIS library, located in the same building. It is a new building, built less than five years ago to replace the older structure affectionately known as the 'cage'. The new 'cage' (the name is all that remains) is a modern, well-equipped building with warm showers, stores, lecture rooms, offices and a library. The library is packed with information concerning the Legion, its history, training and Regiments, written in every conceivable language. According to the Major commanding CIS, 'The information given at the *Centre de Sélection et Instruction* is very important. We do not want the men proceeding to Castelnaudary with any false impressions.'

The modern Legion goes to great length to make sure the EVs fully understand the commitment they are about to make; neither the French government nor the Legion have any wish to waste time and money on volunteers who will soon become disenchanted, be officially discharged or, worse still, desert.

In recent years the Legion has become increasingly selective and has had little problem in maintaining its manpower levels as set down by the French government.

A bugler at Aubagne. Volunteers to *la musique*, the Legion's band, must undergo the same basic training at 4 RE in Castelnaudary as other recruits.

High unemployment among many European nations coupled with operational inactivity among many NATO and overseas armies have led to a large number of volunteers. The *Légion Etrangère* can afford to be choosy. During the last decade thousands of aspiring legionnaires have been turned away by the Legion. For instance, the fall out figures for September 1984 show that only 4% of those who volunteered made it through to the end of basic training. Statistics vary with each intake but an average of around 90% of initial applicants failing to make the grade for one reason or another is not unusual.

The Institution has its own vineyards and few EVs miss sampling a glass

A number fall out after the Intelligence Tests, the first hurdle to be taken by the aspiring legionnaires. The *niveaux générales*, a three-part written general knowledge paper, takes its toll of the less well educated. The *sécurité* interviews by BSLE account for still more, for the Legion will not accept recruits with a criminal record. Those that remain and join *2e section* spend a full week at Aubagne prior to their onward transmission to Castelnaudary and the training battalion. The programme varies from intake to intake but generally goes as follows:

Friday. Morning: Section attends the tailors, where the men are measured and fitted for their uniforms. During their time in Aubagne the EVs are issued with old, well-worn *tenue de combat* and track-suits, but receive properly fitting new uniforms before they depart. Afternoon: Further orientation and aptitude tests, to assess the individual's suitability for specialist skills.

Saturday. Morning: Section visit to the *Invalide Institution de La Légion Etrangère* (IILE) at Puyloubier, to meet and talk with the former legionnaires in residence. The Legion sees this not simply as a break for the recruits, but as an opportunity to emphasise the Legion as a 'family', to show them that the Legion looks after its own, caring for those who have suffered in its ranks. The IILE has its own vineyards and few EVs miss sampling a glass or two of wine. Puyloubier is less than an hour by coach from Aubagne but the visit lasts a full day.

Sunday. Morning: Section divides up into teams for sport, such as volleyball, or goes out on a short run of about three kilometres, wearing running shoes and track suits.

Paratroopers of 2 REP form up on the parade square at Camp Raffalli, near the seaside resort of Calvi in Corsica.

Afternoon: The afternoon is free for rest and relaxation. The bar is open — but for soft drinks only.

Monday. Morning: Section sport, usually a short run of about four kilometres, but slightly less if the EVs spent Sunday morning playing volleyball rather than running. This is followed by a photo session to get each man's picture for his ID card. Afternoon: Solde or pay parade. Legionnaires are paid in cash until they get their original name back or reach the rank of corporal.

Tuesday. Morning: Section attends the medical centre for vaccinations against common diseases. The Legion system is to deliver these immunisations all at once and get them over and done with. Afternoon: The Section undergoes what is termed as *anonymat*. The EVs visit the personnel office and, should they choose, have their names changed, adopting a new identity until, at the discretion of the Legion, their old one is returned.

Legionnaires are paid in cash until they get their original name back

Wednesday. Morning: Section Sport, a road run of between five to six km. This time the EVs run in *tenue de combat*, combat kit, for the first time. Afternoon: The Section visits the *Centre Permission de La Légion Etrangère Malmousque* (CPLEM) — the Legion's R&R centre, situated on the outskirts of Marseilles. The short visit gives the EVs a taste of the kind of nights out they can expect to experience after completing basic training.

Thursday. Morning: Section visits the clothing stores and the EVs receive their *paquetage* — their kit issue, containing almost everything they will need in their five years' period of service. Afternoon: The signing of the initial enlistment or engagement contracts. The EVs also get the chance to look around the Legion museum. This is the men's last day at Aubagne and, if they are musically inclined, they are given the opportunity to undergo the band test for service in *Musique*.

Friday, 0530 hours: Section departs by train for Castelnaudary and their four months of basic training with 4 RE.

For the *engagés volontaires* Aubagne has been part of a transitional process between being a civilian and setting out on the arduous path towards becoming a legionnaire proper. The physical and mental moulding has already begun, but it is now about to be dramatically increased during the harsh, back-breaking training they will undergo at Castelnaudary.

NO FRENCHMEN HERE

Once the Legion has accepted the volunteer, he must earn the famous *képi blanc* by enduring the rigours of an exceptionally tough and thorough basic training course. In this four-month period, as the recruits are gradually turned into soldiers and are forced to the limits of their endurance, more than a few of them will come to regret their decision to become legionnaires.

On their arrival at Castelnaudary the *engagés volontaires* cannot but be impressed by their new home. The camp, Quartier Capitaine Danjou, is a well-designed modern complex built outside the town, and has replaced the older barracks within Castelnaudary itself. The old camp, somewhat dilapidated and now due to be sold off by the Legion, is used for NCO and specialist training. For those EVs who have served in other armies it comes as something of a surprise to find that the recruits have the better deal at the *Ecole de la Légion Etrangère*.

4 RE, the Legion's training regiment, is organised into a command post, a headquarters company and five com-

Live firing advance-to-contact: legionnaires of 4 RE practise their battle skills under realistic conditions.

panies. The first two companies are the *compagnie d'instruction des cadres* (CIC) and the *compagnie d'instruction des specialistes* (CIS). CIC is responsible for training all the Legion's corporals and sergeants, and runs the basic and advanced infantry courses for all NCOs. CIS on the other hand runs the specialist courses for 'mechs., techs., sigs., and medics.' The three remaining companies are the *compagnies d'engagés volontaires*, each one divided into four training platoons or sections.

Each Friday a new intake of between 20 to 35 EVs arrives from 1 RE at Aubagne, and every fortnight a new section forms up to begin its four months of basic training. The size of each new section varies, but the mini-

Tension shows on the face of this *engagé volontaire* on the basic training course at Castelnaudary.

Above: Members of the guard at Quartier Capitaine Danjou in Castelnaudary, one of the Legion's most modern camps. Following pages: The high-point of 4 RE's assault course.

mum is 40 and the average is over 50. The EVs who have made it to this stage represent a mere one out of four volunteers who initially applied to join the Foreign Legion. The initial 'filter' that weeds out the unsuitable applicants was the recruiting sous-officier at one of the Legion's Information/Recruiting Offices. The next stage of selection was conducted at Aubagne where the volunteers underwent medical, physical and intelligence tests. Then the prospective legionnaires had to satisfy the security branch that there was nothing in their past that would prevent their application to join the Legion from being approved. Finally, the EVs make it to Castelnaudary,

where they now have to prove themselves physically and mentally capable of becoming trained legionnaires. They have four months in which to do it.

The EVs' training is divided into four separate, one-month phases. The first month, spent on one of the Legion's farms, concentrates on basic military skills and introduces the section to the Legion system. During the second phase at Danjou the section undergoes more intensive instruction and over the third is introduced to mountain warfare and to small unit tactics. The last phase includes a number of tests, military, physical and medical, at the end of which the individual volunteer's aptitude is assessed, and arrangements are made for his future career within the Legion — if he has made it through the whole shattering process.

Each section is divided into four *groupes* of 10 or more EVs. Usually a section is commanded by a young lieutenant, but one section per training *compagnie* is led by an experienced *sous-officier*. The *compagnies d'engagés volontaires* are mainly self-supporting, with their own vehicles and training stores. Each *section* has eight drivers, two for each of its four trucks. The training *compagnies* have their own transport, unlike most similar units in other armies, and are equipped with SIMCA 4x4 trucks. These ageing French-manufactured vehicles have a fully-laden weight of 5 tonnes, and a troop-carrying capability of 2 + 10. They are driven by EVs selected and trained from the first intake to arrive from Castelnaudary.

At first there is little of the military 'bullshit' associated with basic training

This is the first time that the EVs come across the fact that the Legion does employ skills acquired previously. A man's experience and natural ability does not go to waste. If he was previously an HGV driver he may well find himself driving a section vehicle, in the same way that a cook might find himself spending more time than his fellows over the stove and a nurse might take on the role of section medic.

The *Ecole de la Légion Etrangère* has the use of three farms, one for each of its training companies. 'Bel-Air' is used by the *1e compagnie*, 'La Jasse' by the *2e compagnie* and 'Raissac' by the *3e compagnie*. In addition to the individual compagnie farms there are two others: 'La Ganguise', situated on a lake and offering amphibious training; and 'Camurac', located in the Pyrenees and used for mountain warfare and ski training.

The farm buildings are large, clean and have been thoroughly re-constructed over the past few years. The Legion has replaced leaking roofs, installed proper kitchens and washing facilities, and has even put in central heating. The EVs live in *groupes*, each with its own room complete with bunk beds, bedding and metal lockers, one per man. The corporals and *sous-officiers* responsible for training live with the EVs, although they have separate sleeping accommodation, their own small kitchen, and a bar/rest area which doubles as a briefing room. Only the platoon commander, the *chef de section*, has a room to himself, and this serves as his office as well as his bedroom.

Punishments are exacted for failing to sing one of the Legion's songs correctly

There is little doubt that the EVs are better off than the recruits of many other armies when it comes to amenities. In addition to their own dining area, wash rooms and showers, there are lecture rooms, stores and an armoury. Apart from being responsible for cooking their own meals, which are prepared centrally by EVs detailed on a rotational basis, and keeping their kit, rooms and the living area clean, there is little of the military 'bullshit' that is normally associated with basic training. But the Legion is punctilious about cleanliness and order, so lockers must be properly laid out, and bedding made up into 'biscuits' with the sheets rolled and crossed diagonally over boxed blankets.

There are no regimental duties for the EVs during the first phase, and much of their time is devoted to reaching the high standards of physical fitness demanded by the Legion. Life can get very tough indeed as they undergo a crash course in military discipline and physical exertion. They have to get used to the idea of having little sleep, as their time is taken up with marches and inspections. Punishments are exacted for the most trivial offences, such as failing to sing one the Legion's many songs correctly, untidiness, low standards of personal hygiene or a general lack of effort.

This harsh routine is designed to force the men to think and act like legionnaires. At Aubagne the EVs undertook some road runs, but these were fairly limited in length,

Above right: Recruits practise unarmed combat training.
Below right: An EV section under an Austrian NCO sets off to complete the day's march across the Pyrenees.

the maximum being around six km wearing combat dress; at the farm the EVs begin a fitness programme which involves daily runs and weekly marches. These progress in length from 10km at the beginning to 50km at the end of the fourth week. Even the 'easy' ones can be punishing, such as an eight km cross-country run in full combat kit, helmet, rifle and webbing — while carrying a 35lb rucksack — which has to be completed in under an hour.

There are French lessons every day for the entire four-month period

Orders are given in the French language from the beginning of training, and there are French lessons every day for the entire four month period. For a foreign recruit with no previous military experience it is perhaps easier as he is learning new words for equipment, weapons and procedures with which he is unfamiliar. But to a non-French speaking EV with previous military experience the

The vineyards at Puyloubier, the Legion's retirement home. Wine grown here is bottled under the Legion label and is drunk wherever the Legion serves.

transformation is slightly more complicated; a German volunteer will continue to think of a fusil as a 'gewehr' whereas the Brit will call it a rifle whether it is a French FA MAS, or a British SLR or SA-80.

Singing plays an important part in learning the French language, and the Legion traditionally sings songs on the march, at mealtimes — in fact, at any time the mood strikes them. During training the mood is controlled by the instructors, who will detail either an individual EV or a group to give a rendition of a Legion favourite. Throughout this process those who do not speak French will be helped by those who do. As the average section

Legionnaires on the run, wearing field equipment. Inter-company and inter-regiment competitions, such as this one, play an important part in the training cycle.

includes between 20 to 30 French-speakers the volunteers are paired off, one EV giving the lesson, the other learning. This plays a key part in the integration of EVs into the Legion 'family'. While at the farm the recruits form up into basic 'cells' first as a pair, one French-speaking recruit to one foreigner, then as a *groupe*, and finally as a *section*.

The *chef de section* is responsible for all men under his command

The system during the early stages of training is designed to be formal yet flexible. The corporals who help each *groupe* with its training are usually attached to gain experience in instruction prior to attending their sergeant's course. Most will have served between one and three years with the Legion, although some will have been specially selected for corporal immediately after their own EV training. In the French armed forces there is a distinction between *moniteur* and *instructeur*. Both are grades of instructor but the more junior *moniteur* positions are

The tough terrain of southern France is exploited to the full in the Legion training programme. Officers and NCOs always lead the way, however arduous the activity.

taken up by corporals whereas the more senior slots are reserved for sergeants. At Castelnaudary the corporals instruct the recruits in many basic military skills while the more experienced sergeants, one per *groupe*, are responsible for discipline, organisation and instruction in the more technical military disciplines.

The *chef de section*, usually a lieutenant, remains responsible for all the men under his command. He will be a young officer, often with less than five years experience, three of which will have been spent at the French military academy at St Cyr, with a further year learning tactics at the French Army's Infantry School. His ability to run a section in the *compagnie d'engagés volontaires* will determine his future career with the Legion. If he makes a good job of it he will go on to better things; should he make a mess of it it will be his last tour with the Legion. These young officers are assessed by the Lieutenant-

Colonel at Castelnaudary's headquarters, who warns new arrivals that to succeed they 'must consider their legionnaires as the means, rather than the end.' Their commander stresses that the legionnaires come first, and any officer more worried about his own future rather than the welfare and the training of the men under his command has no future as a Legion officer.

The 'bullshit' factor is brought in as the men are taught to look like soldiers

The legionnaires, their corporals, sous-officiers, and *chef de section*, all train together. If there is a route march with full equipment everybody does it. There are no exceptions, apart from the drivers of the support vehicles and one corporal who remains on duty at the farm, manning the radio and looking after the armoury.

The first phase of training ends with a tough 50km route march back to Quartier Danjou at Castelnaudary and is seen as a real test of the EVs' motivation and ability. Their success is celebrated by a ceremony in which they are awarded their *képi blanc*, the traditional headgear of the legionnaire. The ceremony usually takes place after dark and is deliberately designed to make the volunteers feel they are being accepted into a chivalrous order.

With their first rite of passage behind them the EVs spend the following month at Quartier Danjou for the second phase of their training. The volunteers are introduced to company and regimental life for the first time. The 'bullshit' factor is brought in as the men are taught to look like soldiers as well as act like them. Basic instruc-

Getting to grips with the 'enemy'. The defending legionnaire applies an arm lock before following through with the elbow.

tion is intensified and weapons training now plays an important part in the volunteers' daily life. At Danjou there is a 300 metre full-bore underground range which allows the EVs to practise their shooting skills without having to leave the camp. Physical fitness and French language lessons continue as the recruits begin to master drill, weapons handling and marksmanship. They are beginning not only to look like legionnaires, but to feel like legionnaires.

A typical exercise towards the end of the third month will last over three days

The second phase of training ends with a five day visit to 4 RE's base in the Pyrenees. At Camurac (1000m above sea-level) the EVs have the opportunity to release the physical tension that has built up during their three week confinement in Danjou. During the winter months the sections receive instruction in skiing and winter warfare; in summer they learn the basics of rock climbing. Abseiling off the nearby cliffs is a popular pastime at

Camurac, and is also a useful method for the instructors to assess the recruits' confidence. The general atmosphere, despite the military environment and daily combat training, is relaxed and the EVs usually enjoy their short stay at Camurac.

When the section leaves there is another physical test, a march with full equipment of between 60 to 70km. It is the longest and hardest march so far, and marks the end of the second phase of training. The third month, like the second, is spent mainly at Quartier Danjou. Tactical training is stressed during this phase, with the EVs working on collective, rather than individual skills. The *section* manoeuvres in *groupes*, using personal and close support weapons, including LRAC 89mm anti-tank rocket launchers, grenades, rifle-grenades and occasionally 12.7mm (.50 cal.) heavy machine guns. The volunteers are also introduced to night operations. Until this time their nights

Training is conducted with strict safety measures. Below: Hooked on to the high wire. Opposite: Down the death slide wearing a life jacket, with safety boat in attendance.

VOIE

DE

L'INCONSCIENT

BLATTER
DELEZA
JOI

OUVERTE PAR

out have been in bivouacs while on route marches, but now they learn night navigation and movement.

By this time the EVs have become exceptionally fit. They continue to march, with the distances increasing and the terrain becoming more difficult. A typical exercise towards the end of the third month will last over three days. On the first day they will be dropped off, a couple of *groupes* at a time, in the foothills of the Pyrenees. They will then march south, gaining altitude, covering a distance of between 10-15km before breaking for lunch. During the afternoon they will cover a further 10-15km and set up their section bivouac before nightfall. A communal evening meal will be cooked by the EVs and there will usually be a singing session, where Legion songs are sung around a large fire, before the recruits turn in for the night. At 0400h the following morning the volunteers will rise, pack up their shelters, get their coffee on and load up the section support vehicle. By 0530h,

while it is still dark, they will be ready to move off, higher into the mountains.

Two groups, one led by the *chef de section* and the other by his senior NCO, will leave the night's base camp at 15 minute intervals. Depending on the route and the distance covered, the EVs will arrive at their next halt around four hours later. The route chosen by the *chef de section* will include mountain roads and paths, all of which work their way steadily uphill, the idea being to get the worst part of the day's march over with early on. The normal distance for the first march of the day is about 15km, with an altitude gain of around 600 metres.

After a break of an hour to an hour and a half the section will set off again, still in two separate groups, for the second march of the day. By the time they reach their night bivouac area they will have covered a further 15-20km, most of which will have been uphill. The night routine will be the same as the previous evening, setting

Winter conditions in the Pyrenees and the Alps are ideal for mountain and winter warfare, both of which play an important part in basic and continuation training.

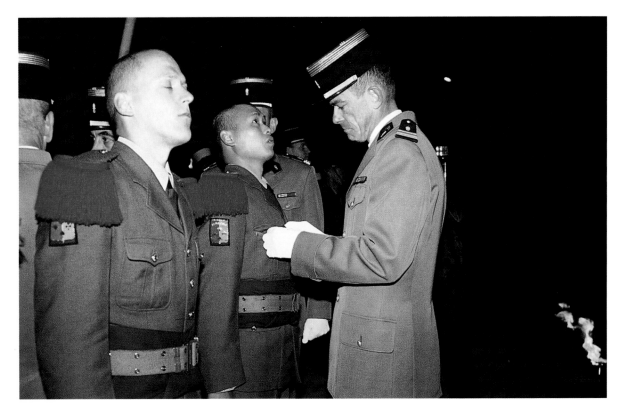

up the bivouac, preparing the meal and resting the weary muscles prior to setting off again before first light.

The two groups will usually meet the section vehicles that will transport them back to Castelnaudary at around mid-day, after they have covered another 20 or so kilometres. The pace is fast and, depending on who is leading the group, furious. Like all other forced marches this is seen as a test. It is more difficult for the EVs than for the instructors, not because the former are any less fit, but because of the ever present fear of failure, which would result in them letting down the other members of their section.

By this time, each volunteer, regardless of where he comes from, or whether or not he is the only one from his race in the section, abhors the idea of letting his side down. Individuals and groups compete against each other to prove that they are the best. One only has to look at the composition of an EV *section* to get an idea of the wide variety of backgrounds from which these men come, and to appreciate the work needed to weld such disparate nationalities into a fighting force with a common purpose. In May 1990, a typical section of 4 RE was composed of the following nationalities:

Ireland (Eire)	1
Britain	3
Switzerland	9
Monaco	4
Canada	5
The Netherlands	2
Poland	4
Hungary	2
West Germany	1
East Germany	1
Spain	1
Malagasy	1
China	1
Japan	1
North America	2
Bolivia	1
Peru	1
Turkey	1
Zaire	1

giving a total of 42 men from 16 different nations including (and unofficially) France. (Although there are 19 nations in the list, most of those registered as Swiss were, in fact French, as were those from Monaco, and three of the five Canadians). However, despite the French elements, the majority of this section was foreign.

By the beginning of the fourth and final month of basic training the volunteers are beginning to think of themselves as legionnaires, first and foremost, and as foreigners second. They now have a firm group identity. French has become their first language, at least as far as work is concerned, and while the majority of EVs are not fluent in the language, they can make themselves understood and do understand most of what is said to them.

They cease to be *les jeunes* (the young ones) and become legionnaires

The fourth phase of basic training concentrates on assessment and tests, and on determining each individual's immediate future with the Legion. The EVs receive lectures on the specialisations available within the Legion, and are advised of their prospects of going to the unit of their choice. They are given their final instruction for their *Certificat Technique Elémentaire* (CTE/00) — the figures representing the motorised and foot infantry specialisation, *élémentaire* being the basic standard.

The final exercise is conducted in the penultimate week of the fourth phase. It is a test that takes the form of an approach march, followed by a raid in which all individual skills are tested. The march lasts for three days. It is an especially arduous one, of between 150-160km, across some of the most difficult terrain in the region. After the raid the EVs must demonstrate their skill in marksmanship in what is known as the *cent cartouches* or '100 rounds'. Each man receives 100 rounds of live 5.56mm ammunition for his FA MAS assault rifle, and must use them all to prove his ability with his personal weapon.

For the remainder of RAID CTE/00, the EVs' Test Week, the course must successfully complete a series of examinations which include skill-at-arms, weapons-handling, marksmanship (with section weapons), setting up an observation post (OP), giving a verbal report, first aid (*secourisme*), radio procedure (*transmissions*) and knowledge of the field manual (*règlement*). The French military still work very closely to the book and *règlement*

EVs on parade at the end of basic training. The course has been hard but, for those who have made it through, the satisfaction of becoming a legionnaire is enormous.

plays an important part in both their training and their combat operations.

Once the EVs have taken and passed all these examinations they cease to be *les jeunes* (the young ones) and become legionnaires. They receive the coveted CTE/00 and return to Castelnaudary. During their final week at Quartier Danjou the newly-qualified infantrymen undergo their final medical tests and are presented to the colonel of 4 RE. By this time the list of spare positions to be filled by the former EVs will have been received from Aubagne. Each individual legionnaire's choice will be respected, and every effort made to get him into the unit he wants to join will be made.

Despite these efforts there are occasionally disappointments. For instance, a man may wish to join the engineers of 6 REG, but may not have the required technical skills. Or it may be that a legionnaire, formerly a paratrooper in another army, is desperate to join 2 REP. He is suitable but there are no vacancies for the next six months. In the former case, other possibilities would be suggested, but in the latter it would be an occasion for using the flexible, informal approach, adopted by the hierarchy of the Legion 'family'. The colonel of 4 RE, or another staff officer, would telephone the commander of 2 REP and explain the situation. Would it be possible to make an exception and create a space? Such personal appeals seldom meet with a negative response.

The months of training have produced legionnaires ready to die for France

These four months of training at Castelnaudary have turned a varied collection of men into legionnaires ready to die for France. Basic training has been hard. For a handful of men the course will have proved to be too much, resulting in their desertion. Many others will have been rejected by the Legion, either through injury or because the rigours of training have revealed a previously undetected unsuitability for the life of a legionnaire. The rest will have become part of an elite, members of *la famille légionnaire*. The men with whom they have completed their training, who may have come from countries they had never even heard of less than half a year ago, are now their brothers-in-arms. They are all ready to be posted to individual regiments which may take them to Djibouti or the Pacific. From Castelnaudary they return to Aubagne to receive their individual postings, where the next stage of their new life is about to begin.

LIFE IN THE LEGION

Fresh out of basic training, the new legionnaire may find himself posted as far afield as the deserts of Djibouti in Africa or the jungles of Guyana in South America. Wherever he is, he must fit in to the Legion 'family', learning to work hard and, on his rare days off, play hard as well. Those who do not fit in can find that life in the Legion may get very tough indeed.

By the time the volunteers leave Castelnaudary they are *Légionnaires, 2e classe.* Having passed their CTE/00 they are now qualified for service with any regiment within the Legion and, although there will usually be other examinations to pass — tactical, technical and perhaps promotional — the newly qualified legionnaires at least have a foot on the bottom rung of the ladder.

At Aubagne they receive their final orders before being posted on to their respective units. In recent years this stop-over has also given the Legion the chance of confirming that the volunteer is fully committed to serving the remainder of his five-year contract. It is also the man's last chance to get out, without resorting to deser-

Life in the Legion is certainly not all hard work. Legion officers, in particular, enjoy a high standard of living when compared to other armies.

tion, or without making a formal application to the Legion's commanding general, a complicated procedure that is reputed to stand as little chance of success as gaining an audience with the Pope.

Aubagne is also used as a staging-post for all legionnaires returning from overseas postings. This practise serves a dual purpose. First, it allows the Legion's administration department to process the individual's personal documentation. Second, it provides the opportunity for the medical department to make a thorough assessment of a legionnaire's health. For the legionnaires arriving from their basic training at Castelnaudary the medical is usually little more than a formality. It is unlikely that the newly-qualified legionnaires will have had the opportunity to acquire some of the more exotic tropical diseases that are prevalent in some of the Legion's far-flung operational areas. But there can be problems, as a doctor serving with 4 RE explains: 'The physical aspects of training here are exceptionally demanding. I have seen 36 stress fractures in the last year — it is very difficult to identify

the exact cause but, left untreated, such injuries can recur and become a major problem.'

Such stress-related injuries are usually diagnosed by the unit's medical officer, but there are others that are more difficult to identify. The well-equipped medical centre at Aubagne regularly runs a barrage of tests on legionnaires in transit. The doctor continues: 'Hepatitis is also a big problem, especially overseas. Hepatitis A is mostly caused by drinking bad water while Hepatitis B is contracted either by sexual liaisons with an infected party or by blood infections, usually acquired by the legionnaire being tattooed with dirty needles.'

The legionnaires arriving from Castelnaudary will have had little opportunity to contract sexually transmitted diseases during their basic training, and the tattoo parlours in mainland France, like the unofficial bordellos, usually

The Legion adheres to the belief that an army marches on its stomach, and France's elite goes to great lengths to make sure that its men are well provided for.

conform to far-stricter standards of hygiene than those the legionnaire is likely to encounter overseas.

Once they have been passed fit the legionnaires assemble in small groups and await their travel documentation and the transport that will take them to their destination — their first real posting in the Legion.

The Legion has a reputation for hard fighting, drinking and fornicating

France goes to great lengths to look after the physical well-being of its legionnaires. They receive first class health care, which they undoubtedly need when one considers some of their postings, their rations are excellent compared to those of most other armies, and certainly of a higher standard than those received by many other French formations. Their uniforms — combat, working and parade — are all smart and practical. The FA MAS 5.56mm assault rifle, the personal weapon of most legionnaires, is efficient, effective and accurate.

Pay is good, better than that of most of France's European allies. Legionnaires do not pay for either accommodation or food, and while *sous-officiers* pay mess bills, these are certainly well covered by increased pay and additional allowances. The standard of life is good for both legionnaires and non-commissioned officers alike, and while living accommodation and off-duty facilities in postings such as Chad and Djibouti leave much to be desired, the extra pay received by Legion personnel during their tours, which usually last four months, compensates in part for their hardships.

Life on operational tours has never been easy for legionnaires, but then few enlist under the misapprehension that it might be. They join the Legion to soldier, and France gives them the opportunity to do just that. The French policy of using professional rather than conscript troops to help police its former colonies, and to provide its overseas bases with adequate defence, leads to the Legion and a handful of other units being allocated both the best and the worst postings abroad. The Pacific atolls are well situated for those who wish to while away their time under the sun, while those who want adventure can brave the less-hospitable climes of Chad or Djibouti.

The Legion has a reputation for hard fighting, drinking and fornicating; while their may be a lull on the operational front, there still remains the opportunity to practise skills in the other two areas. Legionnaires who have not achieved *rectification* — that is, received back their origi-

Two happy legionnaires pose with souvenir *képis*. While life in the Legion is physically demanding there are still plenty of opportunities for the men to relax and have fun.

nal identities — are effectively confined to camp, or at least the nearest town. Unless they are *sous-officiers* or have achieved the rank of *caporal-chef* they may not own a car, or walk out in civilian clothes.

The only feasible method of circumventing the dress regulations is to leave in civilian clothes by a route other than the front gate. This poses a number of problems. First, non-rectified legionnaires should not own civilian clothes. Second, if you are based in a rural area and need transport into town, the only way to get there is by pick-

An inter-regimental relay race at Castelnaudary. Competition is fierce in such events, as EV companies' reputations depend on putting in a good performance.

ing up a taxi outside the front gate. And, finally, by being in town dressed in civilian clothes the legionnaire runs the risk of being picked up by the Legion's *Police Militaire*, the PMs. For all but the most foolhardy the risks outweigh the benefits, and the majority of legionnaires are prepared to hit the town in uniform, or stay in camp and have a few beers in their *foyer*.

Staying in the quartier is the easiest option. If a legionnaire wants to drink in the *foyer* he can do it wearing normal working dress, a track suit or sports gear, but if he wants to leave the camp he has to change into walking-out dress. According to a Scandinavian corporal serving with 6 REG, getting ready for a night on the town is quite a performance: 'It takes half an hour at least to iron and put insignia on a uniform. It isn't worth it. Time-off is pretty restricted as it is.' The corporal goes on to say that unless it is a weekend he would not usually consider going out, and in 6 REG they work during most weekends. 'Saturday morning off is like Christmas here. We

don't often work on Sundays in the Legion, but we should have at least one Saturday off per month. Here we're lucky if we get that.' Some units, such as 1 RE, get every second Saturday off, but it is a Legion tradition to work at weekends, and most regiments stick to the old ways. The remainder of the French Army, regulars and conscripts alike, do not work either Saturday or Sunday.

A pastime of the legionnaire is the pursuit of the fair sex

Despite the corporal's feelings about working on Saturday or the effort involved in preparing to go outside the camp, things are easier today than in the past. An English *adjutant* explains: 'In the old days, even five years ago, we used to check the dress of all legionnaires leaving the quartier. They had to have the correct uniform, properly pressed, and be carrying a sewing kit with spare buttons etc., and a clean white handkerchief. Now it is different. We have been told not to be too strict.'

With the exception of authorised leave, free time is fairly limited and the legionnaires tend to use it fully, if not altogether wisely. Drinking is a traditional pastime,

and providing a legionnaire can still stand up reasonably straight, come out with the required military courtesies, and be sober enough for his duties in the morning, he is breaking no rules. The other traditional pastime of the legionnaire is the pursuit of the fair sex which, as often as not, is undertaken simultaneously with the search for a decent beer or two, preferably Kronenbourg 1664.

Brutality, once a traditional part of life in the Legion, has been reduced

Drink and women, smart uniforms and discipline, are all traditional aspects of Legion life. However, like many military formations, the Legion has changed in recent years, changes that are seen by some as for the better, by others for the worse. In days gone by, discipline within the Legion was rigidly enforced with the occasional use of the booted foot, the fist or some handy inanimate object. Blows were regularly administered to those men either unable or unwilling to conform to the high standards of discipline or of performance required of them. In addition to this 'unofficial' method of punishing erring and ill-disciplined legionnaires there was also, until

Members of the band are excused many of the normal duties of the legionnaire. They are the public face of the Legion, and have to maintain very high standards of performance.

recently, a 'punishment' battalion based in Corsica.

This penal unit was reserved for the continual offender and had a well-deserved reputation for brutality. Today, discipline within the Legion relies on the ability of its NCOs to reinforce their position of authority without resorting to acts of violence. Brutality, once considered a traditional part of life in the Legion, has been considerably reduced, if not altogether eradicated, since the Legion's arrival in mainland France. Public opinion, political pressure and changes in society in general, have led to the implementation of a less rigid system.

In training there still may be the occasional slap around the side of the head or a kick up the backside. According to the second-in-command of 4 RE, the employment of such 'positive motivation' is restricted to experienced *sous-officiers* and would not be used by a corporal or *caporal-chef*. Anyone found misusing his authority in this way would face disciplinary action and be returned-to-unit.

Such restrictions on the means by which a *sous-off* can enforce his authority are seen by many legionnaires as having led to a falling off in overall standards of discipline. An American sergeant explains: 'Things have changed considerably since I've been in the Legion, especially discipline. For instance, I was responsible for taking the legionnaires in my company for lunch today. At the end of the meal I detailed some of them to clear up. One of them refused saying he had something else he had to do. Try as I might I could not get him to work the detail.

'The only option I had was to put him on a charge, involving a lot of paperwork, and he would eventually end up in front of the company commander. Even then

On overseas postings with extreme climates, the Legion's normally rigorous standards of dress may be relaxed.

he would probably get off with it, explaining he was needed elsewhere, getting others to back him up. At the most he would probably get a verbal warning — and that for refusing to obey an order. A slap around the head used to resolve problems like this. Now, hitting a legionnaire means losing a stripe, a reduction in rank.'

'Now, hitting a legionnaire means losing a stripe, a reduction in rank'

The American *sous-off* is not alone in feeling that standards of discipline have dropped in recent years. Many other long-service NCOs share his sentiments. Most agree that the reduction of discipline is mainly due to restricting the traditional means of enforcing it.

Perhaps the last word on the use of controlled violence as it is applied today should go to the Legion's Commandant General who, when replying to 'ill-founded allegations of brutality' said: 'The Legion can be compared to a rugby team. The scrum is tough and highly motivated, and comprises the main offensive element of the team. However it may need to be spurred onwards on occasion, and this can be done by a swift, well-placed boot up the behind, delivered by its coach.'

The relationship between the legionnaires, their *sous-officiers* and their 'coaches' is both interesting and complex. Legion officers continually expound the virtues of 'the family' to visitors, and talk of the special bond between the officers and their legionnaires. According to the present commanding general: 'The bond between Legion officers and legionnaires is totally different to that which exists between the various ranks of other French Army units, and indeed many other armies.'

The fact that the Legion's officers are French does divide officers and men

There is certainly a closer bond between Legion officers and their men than there is between officers, NCOs and soldiers of the French Army, but the general sees things from a different vantage point to many of his sous-officiers and legionnaires. Most have little in common with the Legion's officer corps, which is almost entirely French.

In the 1970s the establishment for 'foreign' officers was one full colonel and one lieutenant-colonel in the entire Legion; one commandant per regiment and one captain per battalion. Bearing in mind that this was at a time when within the *sous-officier* establishment there were 25% more Germans than French, this allowance may not seem generous. Little has changed, except perhaps the prospects of becoming a 'foreign' officer in the Legion have reduced with the passage of time. Today, now that the Legion has become integrated with the French Army, it is unlikely that the French High Command would appreciate senior and middle-management posts going to foreigners. In addition, any prospective non-French officer would have to compete against French Legion officers who are, for the most part, top graduates from the French military academy at St Cyr.

The fact that the Legion's officers are French whereas a large percentage of non-commissioned ranks are 'foreigners', does create a division between officers and men, and those few officers that have come up through the ranks are definitely more respected than their colleagues from the military academies. British legionnaires and *sous-officiers* are particularly outspoken in their criticism

of the French system and its officers: 'They are incapable of taking an independent decision, none of them will accept the responsibility', said one sergeant. 'You only have to look at their battle record over the past couple of hundred years', said another.

'Man-management? There is no such word in the Legion'

These criticisms are aimed at the French in general rather than the commissioned officers in particular, and French *sous-offs* come in for the same 'slagging'. Man-management?' said one English *sergent-chef*, 'There is no such word in the Legion. The French Army has no concept of man-management.' It should be realised that the British

Training in the Legion is incessant and often extremely tough. This river crossing in French Guyana shows how the Legion makes the most of local terrain.

are among the least complimentary of any nationality in the Legion when it comes to remarking on anything French. Indeed, if they are introducing a French colleague to an outsider, they are renowned for prefixing the introduction with a remark along the lines of 'he's French but he's OK.'

The Legion gets some of the best officers France has to offer

In the French military system, which includes the Legion as an 'integral element', promotion within the officer structure depends heavily on performance. A British *adjutant* of many years experience, with perhaps more understanding than a number of his countrymen, explains: 'Each officer wants to create a good impression and when he leaves the unit he wants to have achieved more than his predecessor. This means that if in the two years prior to his arrival his unit trained say 30 specialists, he wants to train 35 to 40. This will look good on his record. He may not be interested in whether they are well-trained or not, he just wants them to pass their examinations. If I start failing people because they are not good enough, he is going to get pissed off.'

On the other hand it should be remembered that the officers that come into the Legion are carefully selected, and throughout their first tour are continually assessed by their superiors. An English-speaking French Legion lieutenant-colonel who until recently was responsible for the assessment of junior officers, sums up the situation: 'A young officer does his two or more years with the Legion and, if he's good, if he fits into the system, he can remain with us throughout his career, or at least come back to us at a later date.'

The Legion's units can be deployed anywhere in the world

Some legionnaires and *sous-officiers* may not think much of their officers, but in this regard they have much in common with the troops of countless armies throughout the world. There can also be little doubt that the Legion gets some of the best officers France has to offer, and some of them have proved very good indeed.

The Legion in which these officers and men serve is an integral part of the French Army, equipped with the same weapons and organised along the same lines into infantry, paratroop, armoured and engineer units. It is an

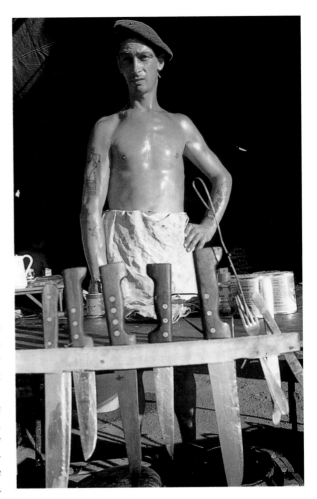

A Legion cook with the tools of his trade. Even in the desert, the legionnaire appreciates good food and drink.

entirely professional Corps, unlike other similarly-sized French formations, and at present has an establishment of some 8200 legionnaires and *sous-officiers*, and 350 commissioned ranks. The fact that the Legion is comprised totally of volunteers means that its units can be deployed anywhere in the world; the French conscript soldier is, by law, not allowed to serve anywhere outside the confines of metropolitan France.

At present, Legion regiments and formations are based in Europe, Africa and South America, with elements in the Indian Ocean and the Pacific. These units come under the control of the Foreign Legion's commanding officer, a two-star general with his headquarters with 1 RE at Aubagne.

The Quartier Viénot is the base of the Legion's central depot, and the home of 1 RE. This regiment, which is the oldest in the Legion and responsible for maintaining its relics and traditions, houses the museum and is the base of the principle band. 1 RE comprises three companies located at Aubagne: the *compagnie de commandement et des services régimentaire* (CCSR), the *compagnie des services de la Légion Etrangère* (CSLE), and the *compagnie administrative des personnels de la Légion Etrangère* (CAPLE). These administrative and support companies provide all other Legion units with a wide range of services and while , predominantly 'desk-bound', would have a combat role in the event of mobilisation.

1 RE also has a fourth company, the *compagnie de transit de la Légion Etrangère* (CTLE), a transport unit based at Fort St Nogent outside Paris, and a small admin-istrative section, the *détachement de la Légion Etrangère de Paris* (DLEP) which works within the French Ministry of Defence. Other detachments, belonging to 1 RE but based outside Aubagne, include three sections of the Moral Department, the *service du moral*, at Marseilles (La Malmousque), Puyloubier, and La Ciotat, two information offices (Paris and Strasbourg) and 15 recruitment offices located across France.

The Quartier Viénot becomes a regular feature in the lives of legionnaires and 1 RE plays an important role throughout their careers. On returning to Aubagne from Castelnaudary the newly-qualified legionnaires are given the run of the camp, and allowed time off, either

A Legion captain makes his point clear to a company of new recruits in 4 RE at Castelnaudary.

evenings in the town or a week-end at La Malmousque, the Legion's rest and recreation centre just outside Marseilles. They have the chance to visit the bars, meet girls and, possibly, get tattooed. Belonging to 1 RE and being a stationed in Aubagne may seem a rather boring prospect to those who have only just graduated from 4 RE, but all agree it is well worth a brief visit.

The *FAR* is France's answer to America's Rapid Deployment Force

Apart from 1 RE at Aubagne and 4 RE at Castelnaudary, there are three Legion combat regiments based in mainland France. These are 1 REC (*1e Régiment Etranger de Cavalerie*), 2 REI (*2e Régiment Etranger d'Infanterie*) and 6 REG (*6e Régiment Etranger de Génie*). These regiments

With its modern role in the FAR, the Legion devotes much time to NBC and anti-tank warfare. These men are training with the LRAC missile launcher.

belong to 6 DLB (*6e Division Légère Blindée*), a light armoured division which is part of the *Force d'Action Rapide*. Known as the FAR, the larger formation incorporates the majority of Legion regiments in one capacity or another.

The *Force d'Action Rapide* is France's answer to America's Rapid Deployment Force. If the French were ever involved in a Falklands-type campaign, it would be the FAR that would be sent forth to deal with it. It comprises five Divisions, in all some 47,000 troops, and can be committed to battle either as a response to a small 'bush-fire' war or, at the other end of the spectrum, as the first deployment response to an overt threat in Europe.

The Legion provides the FAR with a significant proportion of 6 DLB's forward fighting element. 1 REC is one of the Division's two light armoured regiments. Based at Orange, it consists of one headquarters squadron, three armoured reconnaissance squadrons (equipped with AMX 10-RCs) and one anti-tank squadron (with VAB-HOT). 6 DLB also has two infantry regiments, one of

which is 2 REI. Equipped with VAB six-wheeled armoured personnel carriers, this regiment, located at Nîmes, consists of a headquarters squadron, four rifle companies, and two scout and support companies. 6 REG is the Division's engineer regiment. Based at Laudun near the city of Avignon, 6 REG consists of a headquarters company, a support company and three combat engineer companies.

Located outside mainland France is the Legion's paratroop formation

Also belonging to the FAR, but located outside mainland France, is the Legion's sole surviving paratroop formation, 2 REP (*2e Régiment Etranger de Parachutistes*). Based at Calvi, a coastal town at the foot of the Corsican mountains 2 REP is the spearhead regiment of the 11e Division Parachutiste. It consists of a headquarters company, a service support company and four combat companies.

Each of these *compagnies de combat* specialises in a different aspect of warfare. *1e Cie*'s particular specialisation is anti-tank combat and night-time operations; *2e Cie*'s is mountain warfare; *3e Cie*'s amphibious operations; and *4e Cie* concentrates on behind-the-lines actions, including sabotage and sniping. In addition to a Milan anti-tank missile groupe within each *compagnie de combat*, 2 REP possesses its own heavy weapons support including an air-defence section (equipped with 20mm cannon), and two anti-tank platoons (armed with jeep-mounted Milan).

A high proportion of legionnaires are commando trained

2 REP also has a special operations force element, known as *les CRAP* — the *commandos de recherche et d'action dans la profondeur*. The humour of the shortened version is not lost on the English-speaking members of this small, highly select group, but outsiders would be wise to keep any comment to themselves. Known within the Legion as *sauteurs opérationnels* or more simply *sauteurs ops*, these special forces troops are trained in each of the specialist roles of the four *compagnies de combat*. Members of *les CRAP* are military freefall parachutists, skiers, mountaineers, snipers, underwater swimmers and commando instructors. After acquiring these wide-ranging skills these special forces soldiers, for

Overseas tours for legionnaires often mean separation for months on end from family and friends; but the Legion's long home leave periods provide some compensation.

that is what they are, specialise in one of a number of areas: sabotage, reconnaissance, medicine, communications, reconnaissance, motor mechanics etc. Their training is lengthy, intense and rigorous, as befits men who are afforded the same respect from their Corps as members of the Special Air Service Regiment receive from other British soldiers. Not all legionnaires are special forces soldiers or paratroops, but a high proportion of legionnaires are commando-trained, and a number of commando courses are run by the Legion, both within France (at Mont Louis) and abroad (in Djibouti and Guyane).

It is common practice within the Legion for a newly qualified legionnaire to spend his first posting overseas.

Legion mechanics are not only trained to maintain their vehicles, but to manufacture replacement parts — essential when spares may be thousands of miles away.

Four Legion units are permanently based overseas. Some of these postings are in exotic locations, some less so.

3 REI is based at Kourou, in Guyane. The 550-strong regiment mans the border surveillance posts between the neighbouring states of Suriname and Brazil, guards the Guyane Space Centre and is also responsible for the security of the Regional headquarters at Fort-de-France, Martinique. In addition to these duties the regiment continues the Legion's pioneering tradition and is largely responsible for building long stretches of the Trans-Amazonian Highway, a road leading through the dark, dense rain forest that covers the region. 3 REI consists of a headquarters company, two compagnies de combat (rifle companies), and one reconnaissance and support company.

Apart from its normal security duties the regiment also runs the Equatorial Forest Training Centre, near the town of Regina. It is here that legionnaires are trained in the particular 'in-theatre' techniques specific to their operational area. A basic three-day survival course is run at Camp Szuts, a small base camp overlooking the Approuague River adjoining the jungle training area, and covers such topics as shelters, fires, edible plants, trapping, jungle medicine and land navigation. The terrain is difficult, thick jungle slows movement to a crawl, transportation of heavy material and stores can only be carried out by French Air Force Puma helicopters, and the most effective method of inserting patrols is by pirogue, a locally manufactured canoe made from a hollowed-out tree trunk.

The exhausted and hungry teams arrive at their training camp

Tactical training takes the form of the Legion's Commando Guyane, which combines survival training with jungle and military skills training, culminating in an eight day field exercise. The commando course lasts three weeks and candidates are inserted into the training area by pirogue, before marching toward their first objective.

This movement usually takes two days, during which time the course members survive solely on what they can pick up from the surrounding jungle.

'Our goal is to teach them how to survive, move and fight in the jungle'

After surviving on a meagre diet of birds, snakes and fish, the exhausted and hungry teams arrive at their training camp. Over the following days they are instructed in jungle movement, the use of weapons within the jungle environment, and the construction of booby traps, before finally taking part in a land navigation and a live firing exercise.

The aim of 3 REI's jungle commando course is a simple one, as explained by lieutenant Nicholas Kotchine, officer in charge of training during 1990: 'Our goal is to teach them how to survive, move and fight in the jungle.' However, the training itself is far from simple and new skills have to be acquired and old ones adjusted, before

the legionnaires are capable of operating without supervision in this unfamiliar environment.

When the candidates have completed their basic jungle survival training it is time for them to put their new skills into practice. They complete a seven-day tactical movement, across between 40 to 50km of jungle to carry out an assault on a fictitious 'guerrilla' base, carrying on their backs everything they need to successfully complete their mission. The march is both mentally and physically exhausting. Insects provide a constant and real threat to health, and the indigenous scorpions, snakes and centipedes have bites which have been known to prove fatal. If a legionnaire becomes sick or injured the only way out is by helicopter. During the move to the assault position the teams cut out a jungle landing zone for a helicopter, and cross a fast-flowing river before carrying out the

A heavily armed Legion anti-tank patrol returns from a training mission. The LRAC 89 missile system they carry weighs only 8.2kg fully-loaded.

attack. The following day the teams are extracted by Puma to return to Jungle Training Centre near Regina. Successful completion of the course is rewarded by the presentation of the *Commando Guyane* badge. Among those who recently gained their brevet commando were US Marines belonging to Delta Company, 2nd Recon Battalion, based at Camp Lejeune, North Carolina.

The US military is almost always complimentary about the Legion

Reconnaissance marines are among the most highly trained and best qualified of all special operations forces in the Unites States, but even they were impressed by both the techniques taught on the course, and its intensity: 'The survival training was really good. Usually you know it's coming,' explained one marine NCO, who admitted that the Foreign Legion instructors had caught him and his colleagues out on more than one occasion by suddenly springing a survival situation on them: 'I've never faced it like that before, which was great, you didn't know if it was for real.'

His platoon sergeant was equally impressed by the high level of instruction. 'It was a worthwhile experience to work with the Legion in a jungle environment. They are very professional and knowledgeable, and I would recommend as many other Marine units as possible to train down there.' While the attitude of members of the US military towards the Legion is almost always complimentary, the Legion does not always feel the same way about the US forces. The United States of America and France regularly engage in joint exercises in the Mediterranean area. In May 1990 an amphibious exercise involving elements of 1 REC and the US Marine Corps units belonging to the 6th Fleet took place in Sardinia. Although not an amphibious unit as such, 1 REC conducted their beach landings with a speed and professionalism that impressed the American experts. However, once ashore and on dry land the Legion's cavalry were in their element.

Below: A French naval helicopter winches a Legion combat swimmer aboard while a legionnaire looks on from a Zodiac inflatable. Combat swimmers are selected from 2 REP. Opposite: Few commando courses can match the realism of the Foreign Legion's.

The art of combat survival, as taught on the Legion's Guyane Commando Course, brings the legionnaire into contact with some unusual foes.

'The marines seemed very slow, and there was much waiting about on the beach, as if their orders had been lost or they didn't know what to do next,' said one *sous-officier*. He conceded that the Americans were, however, superior to their French allies in one area: 'Their kit is absolutely unbelievable, first class and a lot of it.' One thing that the Legion does share with the US Marine Corps is the opportunity of more exotic postings in the Pacific. 5 REI, for instance, is based in Mururoa and Tahiti. The legionnaires, who include a large element of sappers, are divided between Tahiti, where there is a transit company and an electrical supply unit and Mururoa, where the main body of 5 REI is located. The base at Mururoa consists of one headquarters company, one rifle and one sapper company, an engineer company and a transport and maintenance company.

5 REI provides France's Pacific Experimentation Centre, a nuclear test site, with security, communications, water and power supply, transport and maintenance, and road construction. In fact the Legion's 600-strong detachment on the islands of Mururou and Tahiti are vital to the test site's continued operation. In addition to this role the Legion has undertaken mammoth construction projects which have included building over entire atolls and constructing link roads. They have also built a number of nuclear fall-out shelters both for the space base personnel and for local islanders.

The terrain in Djibouti is as inhospitable as the climate

However, the most common overseas posting for a legionnaire just out of basic training is Djibouti. Djibouti is the permanent home of 13 DBLE, a mixed-arms formation consisting of a headquarters and support company, a rifle company, an armoured reconnaissance squadron and an engineer company. These units are based variously at Gabode, near the capital, and Oueah. 13 DBLE is regularly reinforced by a rotating company supplied by 2 REP, while the other companies are made up of infantry, cavalry and other specialists who are posted in from other regiments on a 'trickle cycle' system. In this way engineers from 6 REG, cavalrymen from 1 REC and legionnaires from the infantry regiments, all get the opportunity for an operational posting. Djibouti is one of the poorest countries in Africa, where it is situated on the 'Horn'. The terrain is as inhospitable as the climate but it is of great strategic importance. And it is also almost ideal for desert warfare training.

Death is a risk accepted by all legionnaires when signing their contract

Unlike Chad, another French-allied former territory, there has been little in the way of actual warfare in Djibouti. Apart from the border incident at Loyada in 1976, where legionnaires faced fire from Somali troops while storming a school-bus held by terrorists to rescue a group of French schoolchildren, there have been relatively few shots fired in anger. Ironically, however, Djibouti was the setting for the worst single loss suffered by the Legion since the Algerian War. On 3 February 1983, a C-160 Transall involved in a parachute training exercise crashed, killing two officers and 27 *sous-officiers* and legionnaires.

Death caused by enemy action, accident or disease is a risk accepted by all legionnaires when signing their contract. However, the chances of being killed in action vary in proportion to the number and intensity of Legion deployments.

Most legionnaires tend to take a fairly fatalistic approach to their continued well-being. Within their first five year contract most will have known at least one colleague who has met with a sudden end, either in a training accident (the Legion follows the 'train hard, fight easy' policy) or while serving overseas on an operational deployment. Death can strike at any time. For instance, in 1985 a *sous-officier* was killed when a bomb was thrown into a bar where he happened to be drinking in Chad. About a month later a legionnaire died after falling from a window at the *Commando de l'Air* barracks at Nîmes, in the south of France.

The idea of the Legion as family holds true wherever a particular unit is posted. Like all families, the Legion often

A Legion sniper crosses a river in Guyana, barely managing to keep his head above water. Legion snipers use the French-manufactured FRF-1 rifle.

finds that disputes between individual members can lead to some leaving the fold. As a legionnaire from 6 REG commented: 'One day you can love the Legion, the next day you can hate it.' And no examination of the life in the Legion would be complete without looking at the topic of desertion.

A high proportion of former soldiers re-engage after their first five years

Boredom has often been responsible for soldiers deserting their armies, and Britain's Army of the Rhine (BAOR), with its endless exercises and lack of any real action, is a prime example. BAOR provides the Legion with a number of volunteers every year. Other NATO armies also supply the Legion with trained personnel, albeit unwittingly. For the most part these men tend to come from the professional, rather than the conscript element of their force.

The Legion prefers recruits who have had previous military experience, but is extremely cautious about

A rainstorm has little impact on a Legion patrol as it moves down river towards its objective in the dense jungle of French Guyana.

accepting soldiers who have volunteered after deserting or have gone absent without leave (AWOL) from other armies. A man who has deserted once may well do it again, and around 50% of those who join the Legion after going absent from another army desert from the Legion. Much depends on each individual's reasons for wishing to join the Legion in the first place. As we have seen, these reasons are thoroughly evaluated when the volunteers arrive at the *Centre de Sélection et Incorporation* (CSI), Aubagne. Here they are given two interviews, known as *intérrogations*, by members of BSLE. It is only after convincing their questioners of their real intent that they are accepted for further training. Those who have left the armed forces of another country for 'political reasons' are preferred to those who desert because of boredom or general disaffection. Many of the latter become 'two-time' deserters, while most of the former recruits,

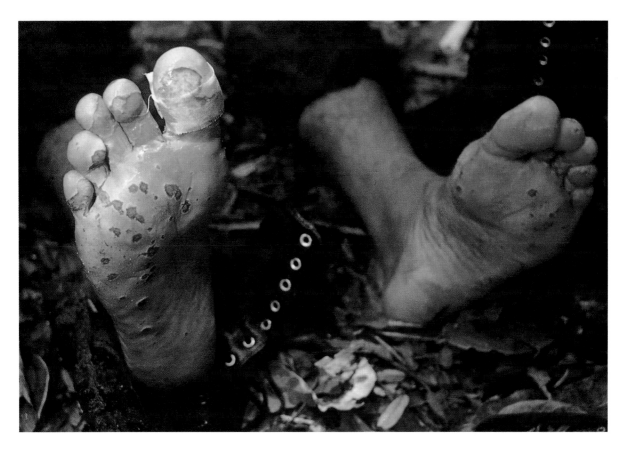

Jungle foot rot can be the bane of a legionnaire's life in the tropics. Parasites, heat and frequent soakings can lead to a number of unpleasant tropical diseases.

often from eastern European countries, tend to complete their contracts.

A high proportion of former soldiers re-engage at the end of their first five years. One such serviceman, now a Legion *sous-officier*, was an NCO technician with the Belgian Air Force before he went absent and crossed the border to join the *Légion Etrangère*. Although his decision to leave his home country was made on the spur of the moment it was not, interestingly enough, made without first having had experience of just what the Legion had to offer.

Uncertainty and challenge defeated repetition and boredom

It transpired that a Belgian Air Force jet had crashed just across the Belgian/French border and the technician was one of a team sent across to France to recover the aircraft. The nearest military post offering temporary accommodation and messing was the Legion recruiting establishment at Lille. The technician, together with his Belgian col-

leagues, ate and drank with the Legion *sous-officiers*, and received what was probably a unique insight into the processing of volunteers, as well as sharing experiences and swapping stories, so gaining a favourable impression of the Legion.

After returning to Belgian the technician had a chance to reflect on his career in the Belgian Air Force, and weigh it up against the opportunities that might be available in the Legion. The latter won out, uncertainty and challenge defeating familiarity, repetition and boredom. He got up one morning soon after his return, packed a small grip with a few personal items, and crossed the border into France.

The friends that he had made among the Legion detachment at Lille did their best to dissuade him, but to no effect. For the next week or so he remained at Lille, drinking and eating with the Legion *sous-officiers* rather than with the group of volunteers that were forming up awaiting transport to Aubagne. He passed his medical examinations, despite the fact that the medic, another drinking partner, advising him to develop some previously unnoticed illness that would prevent him for achieving his ambition. It was no use; his mind was made up. A final drinking session and a word of warning that 'things will change once you've left Lille' from the friendly Legion adjutant, and the new volunteer was on his way to begin his second military career.

He joined the Legion because he was bored and disaffected

Another absentee to join the Legion was a junior NCO from Britain's Brigade of Guards. Unlike the Belgian, he was to become a 'two-time' deserter, leaving the Legion after two years to return to the British Army. Like the Belgian Air Force NCO, he joined the Legion because he was bored and disaffected rather than because he was in trouble with either the civil or military authorities in his home country.

The guardsman was an experienced soldier and he did well in his four months of basic training at Castelnaudary. His request to be posted to 2 REP was accepted and, after completing parachute training in Calvi, he was accepted into the regiment of his choice. However, like many of the British in the Legion, he became disaffected by the French system and when the opportunity arose he 'escaped' while on leave in Paris and returned to the Guards.

Somehow he managed to avoid severe punishment, in the form of a stay at the British Army's 'correction centre' at Colchester, and instead served 30 days local gaol in Pirbright, home of the Household Division. He had returned to the British Army at a time when the Guards Regiments and the Household Cavalry were attempting to gain a foothold in airborne forces and, as luck would have it, was able to transfer across to The Parachute Regiment after completing his basic parachute course at RAF Brize Norton in Oxfordshire.

Already a well-trained infantry soldier, a former NCO and an experienced military parachutist, it was not long before the one-time guardsman and ex-legionnaire regained his rank and, after passing a particularly arduous selection process, joined the Pathfinder Platoon of 5 Airborne Brigade. This led to an unusual epilogue to the former deserter's story.

All Britain's Pathfinders are trained in military free-fall parachuting techniques. These involve jumping from aircraft flying at high-altitude, with the parachutes being deployed at minimum safe height. This leads to the term HALO (high-altitude/low opening), which is used to describe the most common technique of military free-fall.

HALO parachuting is also used as a method of infiltration by the *sauteurs ops*, the elite legionnaire para-commandos belonging to 2 REP's CRAP teams. Both the British and French special forces soldiers use France's airborne training school (ETAP-Pau) which, located in the south of the country, offers good weather for high-altitude parachuting for much of the year. It was at Pau where the ex-Legion paratrooper, now a Pathfinder, bumped into some of his former colleagues from 2 REP, who were more than a little surprised to see him again, especially in France. Their reunion went off without incident and, although the Legion authorities would have been perfectly within their rights to detain him, it is doubtful whether they would have chosen to do so even if they had been aware of his presence. Tact and diplomacy, while not qualities normally associated with the *Légion Etrangére* are, on the other hand, not totally unknown.

The Legion could not, or would not, recognise the fact he had a wife

Some deserters from the Legion return of their own free will. One interesting case in point is that of a Scandinavian, now serving as a corporal signals specialist. During his first enlistment in the Legion he was informed by his family that his wife had died, leaving him with a small daughter. This presented him with a major problem as at the time he had not received his rectification and the Legion could not, or would not, recognise the fact that he had a wife.

Cynics maintain that the Legion withholds *rectification* from married men during their initial five-year contract because to recognise that they had a wife and family would mean that the Legion bore some responsibility for their welfare. Whatever the reason, the Scandinavian legionnaire was unable to gain permission to leave the Legion temporarily, and therefore deserted.

After returning home and making arrangements for his

A modern legionnaire stands guard at the entrance to an ancient fortress in Chad.

A Legion para caught in reflective mood — not surprising, since he has just jumped at low level from a C-160 on to the DZ at Camp Raffalli, Corsica.

young daughter to be cared for by his family, the legionnaire came back to France and re-joined his regiment. He was treated with sympathy by the Legion which, it must be assumed, understood the problem but had been unable by-pass the French military bureaucracy.

The Legion is 'entitled' to shoot a deserter who has taken a weapon

Other deserters can cause the Legion much bigger headaches. One Spanish legionnaire deserted from Djibouti by driving away in his VLRA truck during the night and crossing the border into Somalia. After a period of internment he was released by the Somalian authorities and returned to Spain, a free man. His initial departure had caused a number of problems. Taking a vehicle or a weapon is far more serious than disappearing with a rucksack full of food and water-bottles, and three complete companies had been detailed to search for him once the loss had been discovered. The Legion takes the view that a deserter with a weapon is a potential killer and that they are therefore entitled to shoot him if the opportunity arises.

The deserter himself was later arrested when he returned to France

The vehicle was eventually recovered through diplomatic channels, causing the Legion's hierarchy considerable embarrassment. The deserter himself was later arrested when he returned to France. By this time the man's contract had expired and the Legion were no longer looking for him. Contrary to sensationalist stories in the popular press, the Legion does not seek out deserters, unless the act takes place in an operational area and, more especially, involves a weapon being taken. The Spanish deserter was picked up by the gendarmes for a traffic offence. His name was fed into the national computer and, as the gendarmes are military rather than civil police, his name registered as being a deserter from the *Légion Etrangère*.

Once arrested, he was handed over to the Legion, charged with desertion, and awarded 30 days imprisonment. Had his contract not expired, there would have been a strong possibility of his being returned to his unit to complete the remainder of his five-year engagement. However, the Legion had no further use for him and after serving his 30 days he was discharged and passed over to the French civilian courts, where he was tried for the theft of the vehicle he had stolen in Djibouti.

Legion deserters always stand the risk of being arrested in France if the civil or military police authorities run a check on their identities, a fact that in the past has caught the unwary traveller who, having deserted from the Legion many years past, thinks himself in the clear due to the passage of time. Nowadays, the Legion may not actively pursue deserters, but it does not forget them.

Women have often been responsible for men joining the Legion, but are they also a cause of desertion from the *Légion Etrangère*? As in the past, women play an important part in the life of most legionnaires, although the prospect of marriage is usually far removed from the thoughts of both parties involved.

'The sort of women we meet,' said a British *adjutant*, 'usually belong to the lower scale of French society.' The senior *sous-off* explained that this was mostly due to the legionnaires' position in life, but there were certain advantages to being situated among the lower classes of the social spectrum. 'You can have a good time if you cre-

Family life is not unheard of in the Legion. However, every legionnaire from recruit to general owes his primary allegiance to the Legion, which he regards as his true home.

ate the correct impression. You take them out for a meal, open doors for them, take their coats, seat them first, and stand when they leave the table, and again when they return. You open the car door for them and they're yours. 'Oh Johnny, your manners are so good, I could marry you for them alone.' I don't think that it strikes them that it's a means to an end.'

Sous-officiers, because they are more mobile (unlike legionnaires and corporals they can own cars), have more money and their own rooms, are not as restricted as their subordinates when it comes to meeting a different class of woman. Legionnaires, on the other hand, unable to move far from their barracks, usually end up with professional or at least semi-professional prostitutes. Until fairly recently there were official brothels run by the Legion in mainland France but these were closed down after the government voted against their civilian counterparts continuing their trade.

However, bars located near Legion barracks often cater for needs that go beyond beer and coffee, although of course not officially. For instance, there is the Bar du Pont, situated less than five minutes walk from the Legion camp in Aubagne.

'It offers everything a thirsty, hungry and horny legionnaire could want'

The Bar du Pont has a well-stocked bar, a juke-box, a pool table, bedrooms at a reasonable price and a recently opened restaurant run by a former legionnaire. According to a sergeant in 1 RE, 'it offers just about everything a thirsty, hungry and horny legionnaire could possibly want.'

'Monique', 33 years old and 'non-professional', works during the day as a secretary at an office in Marseilles. Most evenings she catches the train up to Aubagne, gets changed into her 'evening dress' at the Bar du Pont, has a drink and plays a couple of games of pool while waiting for nobody in particular. She has, she says, chosen her 'secondary occupation' partly out of a need to supplement her income, and partly out of her affinity for legionnaires. The extra money she earns goes towards the upkeep of her two children, looked after in the evenings by her mother.

According to Monique, neither her mother nor her colleagues at the office are aware of how she spends many of her evenings. Just what she charges her customers depends on how she feels at the time, and what they can afford. 200 francs gets the legionnaire a 'quicky' while between 500 to 1000 francs will provide companionship overnight, accommodation inclusive.

The Legion still runs two *poufs*, or brothels, outside France

For *sous-officiers* the rate can be reduced slightly if they go back to the quartier. There is a back way from the Bar du Pont to the *sous-offs* mess, avoiding the main gate and guardroom. The code number of the digital access barrier en-route is known to Monique and her colleagues, should their companions be too drunk to remember it.

The professional and non-professional friends of the Legion are accepted as a way of life by both officers and men alike, and this has traditionally been the case. Whereas the *Bordel Militaire de Campagne*, the mobile Legion brothels, and the official 'static' bordellos situated close to Legion barracks are a thing of the past, the Legion still runs two *poufs*, or brothels, outside France, one in Djibouti, the other in Guyane. The pouf in Djibouti is administered by a *capo-chef*, reputed to be one of the richest legionnaires in the country, collecting as much as 7000 francs extra per month.

The legionnaires take a chit as proof they are clear from venereal disease

On pay day the legionnaires receive their money then line up for a medical inspection, take a chit as proof they are clear from venereal disease, and purchase a numbered ticket for the woman of their choice. The official approach is regarded by many legionnaires as being rather too much on the clinical side. You pay your money into the *capo-chef's* black box, then pay a visit to the Legion brothel hoping that the number of your choice is not otherwise engaged. Legionnaires find that at the civilian bars outside the barracks, however, the variety is

Every Legion town has its contingent of the 'PMs' — the military police, who enforce discipline and try to prevent public rowdy behaviour among off-duty legionnaires.

greater and the approach much warmer than in the *capo-chef's* operation.

In Guyane the brothel is staffed by girls recruited by a French civilian entrepreneur and the system operates better than that in Djibouti. It needs to be for, according to the blunt assessment of one legionnaire, 'the local girls are ugly and fuck like shit'. A Legion sergeant's comment about the bordel system as a whole is slightly more considered and revealing: 'I sometimes wish I was an attractive female, one who knew what I know about the Legion. I'd be worth a fortune by now!' Whereas women may sometimes be the reason a man joined the Legion in the first place, they are very rarely the cause of a legionnaire deserting.

The desertion rate in the Legion is very low — less than 5%

Many different pressures can result in a legionnaire deserting. The Legion is a physically demanding organisation, and the initial four months of basic training, undertaken by all volunteers without exception, is long and hard. Some men realise at that this point — unfortunately, already too late — that the life is not for them, and desert. In addition, the legionnaire is bound by a minimum five year contract, the longest minimum enlistment period of any European or American army, and perhaps the longest of any professional military formation in the world. What the recruit experiences in the sometimes harsh reality of everyday life in the Legion may not always match up to the dream that prompted him to join in the first place. Certain legionnaires can find that the pressures build up to such an extent that the only way out of their predicament seems to be desertion.

Because the Legion is reluctant to discuss the matter, and because of sensationalist articles in the popular press, the topic of desertion has become grotesquley distorted and exaggerated. The truth is that the desertion rate in the Legion is extremely low — informed estimates put it at less than 5%. The thorough recruitment process sifts out most of those who are joining for the wrong reasons or who are, for one reason or another, unsuitable for military life. Inevitably, a small minority of misfits slip through the net. Yet this should not lead one to believe that the Legion's retention problems are any worse than those of most modern-day armies. The majority of legionnaires are proud and content to be members of the Legion Family.

INDOCHINA: THE BLOODY YEARS

The Legion was no sooner free of the struggles of World War Two than it was plunged into France's bitter struggle to recover its colonies in Indochina. The long and bloody campaign against the Viet Minh, in which thousands of legionnaires sacrificed their lives, culminated in the courageous defence of the fortress of Dien Bien Phu.

In 1931 the French authorities accorded the Legion a place on the French Army List for the first time in its 100-year history. At the same time, the 'Father of the Legion', General Paul Rollet, was appointed Inspector-General, heading the newly formed *Inspection de la Légion*, the Legion's voice in Paris. Two years later, Sidi-bel-Abbès, the Legion's spiritual home, became the *Dépôt Commun des Régiments Etrangers*, the centre for Legion recruitment. Despite these advances, the Legion's status remained lowly: on the Army List, it ranked below the *Bataillons d'Afrique*, the French penal units.

In October 1939 the Legion consisted of around 15,000 men, whose job it was to keep the peace in the French colonies and undertake much of the manual labour required in their development. These men were divided among six *Régiments Etrangers d'Infanterie* (REI) and two *Régiments Etrangers de Cavalerie* (REC), spread around the French Empire. The bulk of the forces, (1, 2,

3, 4 REI and 1, 2 REC) were concentrated in North Africa, with the balance in Indochina (5 REI) and Syria (6 REI). The outbreak of war, however, brought a flood of volunteers to the regular Legion in North Africa and the Middle East. Many were Germans, who were carefully vetted before being signed on — Nazi infiltration and subversion of the Legion would be catastrophic for France and the colonies.

In France, meanwhile, mixed 'for the duration only' formations were created for the defence of the mainland: 21, 22, and later 23, *Régiments de Marche de Volontaires Etrangers* (RMVE), officered by French Army reservists, were formed from foreign volunteers for the French Army who were living in France when war broke out; and 11, and later 12, *Régiment Etranger d'Infanterie*, trained and

Previous page: Armed with a MAT-49 machine pistol, a bearded legionnaire stands guard over a fort in Indochina. Below: Legionnaires in action against the Viet Minh.

led by Legion officers, was manned by a combination of volunteers from other Legion units and called-up French Army reservists. When the blitzkrieg was turned on France, these Foreign units were waiting. Most took appalling casualties; all quickly ceased to exist. But one recently created Legion formation was destined to escape oblivion and survive into the modern era.

13 DBLE remained with the Allies in the second battle of El Alamein

The *13e Demi-Brigade de Légion Etrangère* (13 DBLE) was formed in Algeria and Morocco in February 1940 to help Finland repulse the Soviet invasion; in the event the formation was sent to Norway in May to aid the Allied cause against Germany. When, in June, the Nazis struck at France, 13 DBLE was recalled, but landed in Brittany just as Paris fell. The Vichy government disbanded the formation but not before one battalion had opted to join

the Free French. Keeping the title 13 DBLE, this unit fought in the Cameroons, the Horn of Africa and against 6 REI in Vichy French Syria, before achieving immortality at Bir Hakeim in the Allied defence of the Gazala Line.

Desperate battles ensued in which the Legion fought to the end

13 DBLE remained with the Allies through the second battle of El Alamein and the drive on Tunisia. Meanwhile the US invasion of Algeria in November 1942 had freed what was left of the Legion in North Africa to join the Allied side. Although the Legion had not been disbanded by Vichy, it had been starved of men and equipment and allowed to run down; nevertheless, the remnants of the North African contingent, plus 4 DBLE recalled from Senegal, had a contribution to make to the ejection of the Afrika Korps from the continent. Later in 1943, 1 REC was brought up to strength and the remainder of the force formed into the *Régiment de Marche de la Légion Etrangére* (RMLE). In 1944, these formations and 13 DBLE assisted in the liberation of France.

As their colleagues in Africa and Europe took up arms against the Germans, the Legion in the Far East continued to endure the Japanese occupation of Indochina. With the exception of one incident in 1940, when legionnaires of the resident formation, 5 REI, had engaged the Japanese over a misinterpretation of the Franco-Japanese agreement on bases, the two sides had not yet come to blows. But on 9 March, with France liberated and the war in Europe all over bar the shouting, the Japanese authorities invited the local French military officers to a dinner at which they were arrested at gunpoint.

The Japanese demand was that the French forces in Indochina surrender. The Legion refused; the Japanese attacked French garrisons in force. A series of desperate hand-to-hand battles ensued in which the Legion fought to the end. Gas was used against one 5 REI fortress in which 60 died, and in at least one incident those taken prisoner were machine-gunned, the survivors of the firing squad then being clubbed, hacked or stabbed to death. On 12 March the French commander, General Lemonnier — who refused to surrender — the French Resident, Camille Auphalle, and Legionnaire Tsakiropolous, a survivor of the massacres who was later recaptured, were taken out and beheaded, having first been forced to dig their own graves. As these events were taking place, the remaining 3000 of 5 REI began a 52-day fighting march to

Yunnan in China. Around 1000 of them made it. The Legion's presence in Indochina, continuous since 1883, came to an end — but not for long.

On 15 August 1945, Japan surrendered and in an attempt to prevent the situation in Indochina from deteriorating into complete chaos, the Potsdam Conference placed the north of the country in the keeping of Nationalist China, and put the British in charge in the south. Almost immediately, however, the British made way for the returning French, who ousted the local Vietnamese administration, which had installed itself in Saigon. The French soon discovered that a return to the pre-war status quo would be difficult — many of the people were unco-operative and, some downright hostile.

In an effort to impose their will, they called in the Legion

The major organisation orchestrating anti-French activities and carrying out attacks on French troops in Indochina was the Viet Minh (Viet Nam Doc Lap Dong Minh — League for the Independence of Vietnam), a communist-led nationalist coalition dedicated to expelling the colonial power. It had emerged in 1941 in the Chinese city of Tienshui as the armed element of the Indochinese Communist Party (ICP), which had itself been formed in the 1930s by Nguygen Hai Quoc. With the rise of the Viet Minh and its crusade against the colonial power, Nguygen Hai Quoc had changed his name to Ho Chi Minh ('He Who Lights The Way'). During the war his forces had been trained and equipped to fight the Japanese by the American OSS. Four days after the Japanese surrender, Ho entered Hanoi and, along with his principal military commander, General Vo Nguyen Giap, set up the Vietnamese government recognised by the Nationalist Chinese. Ho had immense popular support; but the French intended to stay, and in an effort to impose their will, they called in the Legion.

The first Legion unit to arrive back in Indochina was 2 REI, which arrived in Saigon on 2 February 1946. 2 REI had been re-formed on 1 January from the *Régiment de March de la Légion Etrangère en Extrême Orient* (RMLE-EO), which had been created specifically to counter the Japanese threat in Asia. On landing, the regiment was despatched to southern Annam, where it was to reassert French authority; it lost 230 dead and wounded in three months of operations. Also in February, the remainder of 5 REI, the *Bataillon de Marche du 5e Régiment Etranger d'Infanterie* since July 1945, marched out of China and back into Indochina, arriving in Saigon in April.

13 DBLE arrived in Indochina and deployed to Cochin-China and Saigon

On 6 March 1946 an 'Accord' was signed between Ho and the French government by which France undertook to recognise the Vietnamese Republic in the north and the Vietnamese in turn pledged to respect French interests in their country. Under the agreement the French were also allowed to station troops in Tonkin and they took immediate advantage of this to land at Haiphong. That same month 13 DBLE arrived in Indochina and deployed to Cochin-China and Saigon to impose law and order. 3 REI,

Legionnaires inside a village plug their ears as a heavy mortar provides covering fire for friendly forces during a search and destroy mission against the Viet Minh.

re-formed from the RMLE of World War Two, landed three months later and were also posted to Cochin-China.

Although relations were strained between the Legion and the local population and incidents took place involving the Legion and the Viet Minh, open conflict did not break out until the end of 1946. In November, the month in which the Democratic Republic of Vietnam was declared, with Ho as president, Viet Minh guerrilla attacks accounted for 29 French troops. The gloves came off. A French warship bombarded Haiphong, causing 6000 casualties. In late December the Viet Minh launched direct armed attacks on French posts but were beaten off. The guerrillas were more successful in Hanoi, where, after cutting off the public utilities, they killed or kidnapped some 600 French civilians.

By the end of the year, the Legion was at war in Indochina and Ho and the Viet Minh dispersed into the hills of the Viet Bac, beyond the Legion's reach. For although the French were now in control of most of the

south, their influence in the north was restricted to the Red River Delta around Hanoi and Haiphong. Giap knew this and also that he could not defeat the French using conventional tactics.

In 1947, classic low-level guerrilla warfare began

So, in 1947, classic guerrilla low-level warfare began. The guerrillas, operating with the support, or at least the sympathy, of much of the local population (Ho attracted not only communists but non-communist nationalists), were extremely elusive and impossible to eradicate from the countryside. The French, on the other hand, including the Legion, were immediately put on the defensive by being forced to spread the limited forces available over an enormous area of hostile country. Nevertheless, the Legion had its successes, in what was at this point a 'win some/lose some' campaign for both sides.

The French in Indochina were restricted in what they could achieve not only by a shortage of manpower, but also by the limited equipment at their disposal. Although Legion strength in the region was increased in January 1947 with the arrival of 1 REC, this formation was forced to operate on foot until its armour started to arrive in April. In fact, the French armed forces in general were woefully underequipped at this time. In the late 1940s they had little in the way of road transport and the Legion in Indochina had to rely on former American lend-lease jeeps and British lorries. Personal weapons too were of mixed vintage, mostly of US manufacture with some British and French weapons thrown in. The Garand M-1 semi-automatic rifle and Browning automatic rifle (BAR) were preferred weapons because of their high rate of fire,

French Air Force fighters take off from a temporary airstrip in Indochina to provide close air support for the embattled legionnaires on the ground.

While ammunition lasted, heavy artillery played an important part in the Legion's defence of Dien Bien Phu. By the end of the siege, even aerial resupply was impossible.

but as the conflict progressed the MAT-49 sub-machine gun was introduced for close-quarter work. This French-manufactured 9mm weapon featured a sliding wire butt and a magazine receiver which could be rotated 90 degrees to the front to lie underneath the barrel. This meant that the weapon was ideal for use by armoured-vehicle crews, and would later prove so for paratroopers.

The Legion embarked on a 'hearts and minds' campaign

The French plan was not to take the war to the Viet Minh, but to occupy the main towns and attempt to occupy as much of the northern countryside as possible through small detachments of legionnaires, manning forts and carrying out patrols and searches. The forts, often built by the legionnaires themselves, were generally about 30m square, walled with whatever materials were to hand, with a watchtower at each corner and a mortar as their heavy weapon; the 13 DBLE fortress at Hoc Minh, on the

other hand, was a palace, brick-built and with plumbing and electricity. But these outposts had one big disadvantage: they had to be resupplied along roads, so troops were also tied up keeping routes open and providing convoy protection.

As part of their quest to exert control outside the towns, the Legion embarked on a 'hearts and minds' campaign in an attempt to win over the population. The Legion had been well known in Indochina since 1883, yet despite over 75 years of exposure to each others' ways, the Legion's community development programme had failed and the policy of close co-operation had to be abandoned because the Viet Minh carried out reprisals against those to whom the French provided aid. Villagers were tortured and killed by Viet Minh units, and the Legion was spread too thin to offer round-the-clock protection. The Viet Minh did not restrict harsh treatment to compatriots who had fallen out of favour. Castration, disembowelment and even crucifixion could be expected by legionnaires if they fell into guerrilla hands.

In March 1947, 3 REI moved from Cochin-China in the south to the Lang Son area of Tonkin in the north of Indochina, establishing a chain of posts along the Cao Bang-Lang Son Ridge, notably at Cao Bang itself. This area could not help but become a target for the Viet Minh. Early in 1948, Giap focused his attention on the posts in the Cao Bang area, and beginning in April attacks on these forts intensified, culminating in July with the assault on Phu Tong Hoa.

Waves of guerrillas poured towards the outpost to the sound of bugles

Situated in the Cao Bang hills, the fort of Phu Tong Hoa controlled the surrounding area. The garrison commander, Capitaine Cardinal, was aware of an enemy troop build-up in the region and had patrols out when the 316th Viet Minh Division began the engagement with an artillery barrage at 1930 on 21 July. Although the garrison of 104 legionnaires from 3 REI were expecting the attack, the extensive use of mortars, 37mm and 75mm guns surprised them. Shortly after the attack began Capitaine Cardinal was killed, and by 2020 his second-in-command, Lieutenant Charlotton, injured by the same shell, had also died. Command fell to Lieutenant Bevalot, a newly arrived junior subaltern with less than a fortnight's experience of Indochina. Minutes after he had taken over, a shell brought down the radio antenna; communications with the outside world ceased, and though a message had been transmitted moments earlier, advising the nearby post at Bac Tan of the situation, for now, the garrison of Phu Tong Hoa was on its own.

At 2100 the enemy artillery ceased fire, and waves of guerrillas poured towards the outpost to the sound of bugles. They attacked from three directions simultaneously and after 30 minutes of close-quarter fighting,

Garand rifles slung across their shoulders, a Legion patrol crosses a bridge spanning one of the many rivers that criss-crossed their area of operations.

breached the western perimeter, pushing their way into the compound through sheer weight of numbers. Regardless of the heavy casualties they sustained, the Viet Minh continued to press home their attack, but the legionnaires fought back with grim determination. Sergeant Huegin, an experienced Legion NCO, manned a light machine gun (one of only three in the fort) on his own for almost quarter of an hour, holding off the guerrillas until he was killed; Paulen, the radio operator, died at the point of a bayonet while trying to relieve him.

In hand-to-hand fighting there were few to match the legionnaires

Yet when it came to hand-to-hand fighting there were few to match the legionnaires. With three of the four sandbagged corner bastions now held by the Viet Minh, the legionnaires rallied round their NCOs. They fixed bayonets and drove their attackers back across the compound, recapturing first one then another of the bastions. Until this point the battle had been fought in darkness, but now the clouds that had so far obscured the moon began to pass and the area was illuminated; the Viet Minh

withdrew as Legion snipers picked off guerrillas in the final bastion. By 0100 on July 22 the attack was over and the legionnaires were mopping up the few remaining wounded Viet Minh within the compound and around the walls. When reinforcements finally arrived two days later, after fighting their way to Phu Tong Hoa, they found the post almost totally destroyed and two officers and 21 *sous-officiers* and legionnaires dead. Despite this, and to the amazement of Colonel Simon, the officer leading the relief column, the Tricolour still flew from the flagstaff and he was greeted by a guard of honour dressed in *képis*, epaulettes and sashes.

Maintaining fortified outposts across northern Indochina created a massive demand for men. Troops were raised locally from among the Indochinese and placed in mixed units, along with soldiers from other French colonies, notably North Africa and Senegal, and the Legion. These Asians were not granted full legionnaire status and this was reflected in their uniform: they

Loaded down with grenades and spare magazines for their MAT-49 machine pistols, a group of legionnaires pause during a hill patrol.

were not entitled to wear the blue waist sash and they wore a white beret instead of the *képi blanc*, so that they could be distinguished from Asians who had joined the Legion in the usual manner. Locally-raised recruits attended in-country training camps which emphasised the guerrilla warfare in which they would specialise, but the mixed units to which they belonged were not well enough fed or well enough supported to function properly. They fought hard, but sickness rather than the Viet Minh accounted for a large number of their casualties.

The Legion in North Africa was starting to develop a parachute capability

Alongside the Indochinese legionnaires in the mixed units at the start of the campaign were a large number of German nationals, most of whom had served in the Wehrmacht or the Waffen SS. Many of these had distinguished themselves in the service of the Third Reich and some had risen to high rank. Such men (including, it has been claimed, a number of war criminals) had been accepted into the Legion and, as experienced and battle-hardened soldiers, they acquitted themselves well, soon

forming a cadre of *sous-officiers* throughout the Legion in Indochina. In 1948, the Germans were withdrawn from the ranks of the mixed units and a 900-man German battalion was formed. Consisting of three companies, and led by German officers, the battalion carried on its own counter-insurgency war, with considerable success.

As the war began to hot up in Tonkin, the Legion in North Africa was starting to develop a parachute capability. First there was only a company as part of 3 REI, then, in July 1948, the same month that the attack on Phu Tong Hoa took place, the first of the Legion's parachute battalions was formed in North Africa. This was the *1er Bataillon Etranger de Parachutistes* (1 BEP), and by November it was in Tonkin on infantry duties. The following February a second parachute battalion (2 BEP) arrived from the Legion parachute training school at Khamisis, near Sidi-bel Abbès, and began operations in south Annam and Cambodia. In June 1949, 1 BEP absorbed 3 REI's parachute company, and in November, a

Radio communications in Indochina provided a vital link between Legion units dispersed over a wide area in their efforts to root out the elusive Viet Minh.

third battalion, 3 BEP, was raised in Algeria and supplied replacements to the two battalions serving in Indochina.

At first the paras' role was to act as a mobile reserve, either to reinforce French units or deploy to act as 'stop groups' to prevent free movement by the enemy. They soon extended their activities, however. Small groups carried out operational descents as a means of inserting fighting or reconnaissance patrols, and the technique was found to be effective. The Legion was now enjoying more mobility than at any other stage of the war; it had the parachute option, and 1 REC was successfully operating Crab and Alligator amphibious AFVs in the marshes and swamps of the Plain of Tumba in Cochin-China. Based on the US M29 cargo carrier the Alligator Amphibious Tracked Vehicle was fitted with overhead armour and, unlike the open-topped Crab variant, afforded a fair degree of crew protection. Although the French nominally controlled the south, the area was a hotbed of nationalist activity and the Viet Minh, unidentifiable in the mass of the population, moved freely among the packed villages of the Mekong Delta. The French also had trouble with the various non-communist gangs and religious sects operating in the area. This acquisition of amphibious vehicles led to new tactics in the war against the Viet Minh and other groups. No longer restricted to roads and hard ground, the Legion could now pursue the guerrillas into areas which had previously been 'safe'.

The legionnaires carried out a bayonet charge. They were wiped out

Yet the main French strategy remained unchanged: to occupy the countryside by means of outposts. To this end, during the course of 1949, 5 REI, was re-formed and brought into Tonkin to act as convoy escort and carry out building work, and 6 REI was re-formed in North Africa to act as a pool of replacements for the Indochinese campaign. But this increased Legion manpower was as nothing compared with the aid that started to come over the border to the Viet Minh from China, once Mao Tse-Tung had defeated Chiang Kai-shek and his Nationalists in late 1949. Thanks to Chinese instructors and equipment, the Viet Minh evolved into a stronger and more sophisticated fighting machine. From 1950 onwards, Giap had under his command professional troops organised in regular infantry units, as well as guerrillas.

Giap's immediate goal, as part of his plan to control the entire area of Tonkin, was to dislodge French forces from the Cao Bang Ridge and push them back to the Red River. In an action similar in many ways to that at Phu Tong Hoa, Giap attacked the French fort at Dong Khe.

The attack took place on 16 September 1950 and began with an intensive artillery barrage followed by a ground assault spearheaded by six infantry battalions. The defending legionnaires lost three of the four fortified corner bastions and, because of repeated attempts to recover these, found themselves losing men as well as ground. At the end of a long day's fighting the legionnaires had sustained heavy casualties, with 40 dead and 100 wounded. With the enemy closing in to burn the survivors out of the single remaining stronghold, the legionnaires formed up and carried out a bayonet charge. They were wiped out.

Giap's forces continued to their next objective, the fortress at Cao Bang

After their victory at Dong Khe in September 1950, Giap's forces continued to their next objective, the French fortress at Cao Bang. Despite the advice of General Alessandri and the fort commander, Colonel Charton, General Carpentier, the overall commander in Indochina, decided that attempting to hold Cao Bang would be too costly. He therefore ordered the Legion to withdraw, by road, the 80km to the city of Lang Son. The road along which the convoy would have to travel — Route Coloniale (RC) 4 — was known by the French as the 'road of death', because of the frequency and effectiveness of guerrilla attacks on convoys. To provide support to the retreat from Cao Bang, therefore, Groupement Bayard, under Colonel Lepage, was sent up RC 4 from Lang Son with orders to rendezvous with the Cao Bang force at Kilometre 28 near the French fort of Dong Khe.

On 15 September, Colonel Lepage's force left Lang Son and four days later successfully reached the Legion post at That Khe. Dong Khe, however, was firmly in Viet Minh hands by the time Groupement Bayard arrived there on 2 October, and attempts at recapturing the fortress were rebuffed. An attack in strength by the Viet Minh then drove Lepage's column off RC 4 and into the jungle, with 1 BEP acting as rearguard, fighting a running battle with the guerrillas. When the Legion paras caught up with Lepage's force, they found it penned in the Coc Xa gorge. In order to join the remainder of their comrades, 1 BEP had to make a night descent of the almost vertical slopes of the gorge, running the gauntlet of the Viet Minh.

Casualties were high. Over 100 legionnaires of 1 BEP died that night; a further 120 were killed two days later on 7 October as Groupement Bayard attempted to break out of the gorge.

Meanwhile, Colonel Charton's column from Cao Bang was less than two kilometres distant. Since the Viet Minh now held Dong Khe, which dominated RC 4, Charton's force had been advancing along the Quangliet trail, parallel to the main route. The commander, despite being hampered by 2000 civilian refugees, led his combined force of 3 REI legionnaires and Moroccan colonial troops off the trail, and towards the Coc Xa gorge and the noise of battle. It took nearly two hours for his troops to hack their way through the bush and by the time they reached the top of the gorge, what was left of Bayard was in chaos; Lepage himself was fighting alongside the surviving legionnaires of 1 BEP and the troops of the *8e Tirailleurs Marocains* were in a state of disarray. Their panic spread to the Moroccans under Charton's command, while legionnaires of the 3rd Battalion 3 REI struggled in vain to hold the rear. A rout ensued in which both columns were destroyed.

As a result of the actions associated with the with-

American-made M-1944 field howitzers of an artillery battery provide heavy fire support. The Legion made extensive use of American weapons and equipment in Indochina.

drawal from Cao Bang, 1 BEP and 3/3 REI ceased to exist, while 2/3 REI sustained heavy casualties. Charton and Lepage were among those led away into captivity; only a handful of survivors got safely away and made it back to That Khe. Days after the battle at Coc Xa, the French GHQ at Hanoi ordered Lang Son to be abandoned. Lang Son, a modern city, was the last of the French strongpoints on the Cao Bang ridge and the closest to Hanoi and the Red River Delta. The withdrawal was achieved without the loss of life suffered during the withdrawal from Cao Bang, but the loss of face that the French incurred was incalculable. The Viet Minh captured 940 machine guns, 125 mortars, 13 field artillery pieces, 45 soft-skinned vehicles and three armoured cars.

In the wake of the Cao Bang withdrawals, Marshal de Lattre de Tassigny was sent to Indochina as overall military commander and head of the civil administration. De Lattre's plan was to reinforce the French-held Red River Delta through building a fortifed defensive cordon manned by the Legion which became known as the de Lattre Line. Until now the French had failed to persuade the Viet Minh to attack in strength at a place of their choosing, but this line drew Giap to it like a magnet. At the beginning of 1951, the Viet Minh launched three assaults — Vinh Yen, Moa Khe and Day River — all three of which were repulsed successfully. This did wonders for French confidence, but they were unable to capitalise on these victories and the initiative returned to Giap; this despite a major French attack on Hoa Binh by a force which included 1 BEP (re-formed in March 1951), 2 BEP and two battalions of the demi-brigade.

Towards the end of 1951, de Lattre was taken ill and returned home, to be replaced by General Salan. The following October, the Viet Minh attacked and took Ngia Lo, on the ridge which lies between the Red and Black rivers, driving the French off the ridge altogether. Salan mounted Operation Lorraine against Viet Minh supply centres at Phu Thon and Phu Doan with the intention of taking the

ridge back, but the operation failed and Giap was edging nearer to control of the whole of Tonkin. Nevertheless, in November there was a success as 3 REI beat off an attack on Strongpoint 24 at Na San in the Black River valley.

Giap marched into Laos and escaped with the country's opium crop

In the short run this victory served the French cause well, as it cost Giap the best part of a regular division, but in the long term it may have been catastrophically counter-productive. French military thinkers now came to see the isolated base equipped with heavy weapons as a means of curbing Viet Minh operations and banked on the developing art of aerial resupply as a heaven-sent answer to the problem of replenishment. When Giap marched into Laos in April 1953 and escaped with the country's opium crop, the French, in a bid to prevent him doing it again, began to construct a massive fortified airhead in the hills near the Laotian border. The site was a natural bowl which military planners considered would be impregnable from the ground, once developed. It lay around 320km north of Hanoi close to the junction of three roads in northern Tonkin and was named after the nearby village of Dien Bien Phu.

A perimeter dotted with reinforced strongpoints enclosed the airstrip

The decision to build the fortress was taken in July 1953 and the operation to man and develop it (codenamed 'Castor') began on 20 November, as the advance party, paras of 1 BEP, jumped into the Dien Bien Phu valley. Over the next three months a further four Legion battalions (1/2 REI, 3/3 REI, 1/13 DBLE and 3/13 DBLE) streamed into the rapidly growing stronghold, with another (2/3 REI) following close behind. A perimeter dotted with reinforced strongpoints bearing girls' names enclosed the airstrip and formed the main the fortress, while beyond the fence there were four detached, independent outposts — 'Anne-Marie', 'Gabrielle', 'Isabelle' and 'Beatrice'. The Legion troops, which also included two mixed mortar companies, under the command of Lieutenant Colonel Jules Gaucher of 13 DBLE, built and

Fatigue and tension show on the faces of entrenched legionnaires defending the garrison at Dien Bien Phu. Defence of the fortress rested heavily on the Legion and French paras.

held many of these key positions (though their commanders were concerned that they had limited fields of fire and were overlooked), and the paras of 1 BEP were assigned to act as mobile reserve. In addition to the Legion elements, the garrison comprised four battalions of French paras and several battalions of North African and Indochinese colonial troops.

French aircraft began to find the skies hot with enemy anti-aircraft fire

When the decision was taken to develop the fortress at Dien Bien Phu, senior French commanders believed that the Viet Minh simply did not have the firepower or the logistical wherewithal to mount an attack large enough to take it; nor did they believe that Giap would accept an invitation to a pitched battle. Before long, however, it became apparent that Navarre and his staff had severely underestimated the skill and resourcefulness of Giap. French aircraft began to find the skies above Dien Bien Phu hot with enemy anti-aircraft fire — a bad sign when the survival of the base depended on resupply from the air. It was not until March 1954, however, that the full horror of the French predicament was revealed.

Yet Giap's opening gambit was psychological. On the night of 12 March, a small Viet Minh demolitions party infiltrated through the perimeter of the French fortress and bombed the airstrip, leaving propaganda leaflets in their wake. Some of these were written in French and German and advised the defenders that Dien Bien Phu would be their final resting place; others displayed a cari-

Legionnaires scatter as an artillery barrage begins. The Viet Minh heavy artillery was crucial to them at Dien Bien Phu.

cature of Navarre's hand, pushing French soldiers to their doom on to a line of Vietnamese bayonets.

The following day Giap laid his cards on the table. Since the previous December, the Viet Minh commander had been manoeuvring four of his 'regular' divisions into position around the French stronghold; but more than this, armies of pioneers had manhandled artillery and anti-aircraft guns into the very hills whose much-vaunted inaccessibility to such hardware was supposed to protect Dien Bien Phu. At 1700 on 13 March these guns unleashed a murderous barrage on the Legion detached strongpoint 'Beatrice'. Lieutenant-Colonel Gaucher and Major Pegot, commanding 3/13 DBLE, were killed in the bombardment, which was followed by 'human wave' attacks of fanatical ferocity by Viet Minh infantry. By the time the battalion was ordered to quit 'Beatrice' in the early hours of 14 March, 400 legionnaires were either dead, wounded or missing in action. An entire battalion had been destroyed and the battle had only just begun.

This page and opposite: Legion paras go into action in Indochina. Paratroops were often used to reinforce isolated outposts that could be reached in no other way.

On the evening of the 15th, the Viet Minh carried out a similar attack on the strongpoint 'Gabrielle'. This also fell, despite a counter-attack in which two companies of 1 BEP took part.

A lull now ensued in the infantry battle, but the Viet Minh continued with a relentless artillery and mortar bombardment of the main defences and the runway. The incessant shelling proved too much for Colonel Piroth, the French artillery commander; once so confident that he turned down the offer of more weapons, Piroth now held himself personally responsible for the base's plight and committed suicide. Despite heavy shelling, the airstrip remained open for a few days and reinforcements were brought in, among them Lieutenant Colonel Maurice Lemeunier, who replaced Gaucher as Legion commander. It would not be long, however, before the airstrip was unusable and the surviving defenders driven underground. The Viet Minh had begun to tunnel their way forward and had established a series of trenches from which their snipers could pick off the unwary.

Control of the base passed to the colonial para and the Legion officers

In the midst of all this, it was becoming clear to certain Legion and colonial para officers that the overall commander of Dien Bien Phu, Colonel de Castries, an experienced French Army cavalry officer, was having trouble coming to terms with the developing situation. An advocate of taking the war to the enemy, he was out of his element in the kind of last-ditch defensive battle now in progress. On 24 March, a confrontation took place in the command bunker between de Castries and Lieutenant-Colonel Langlais of the colonial paras, one of the disaffected officers.

Control of the defence of the base passed to the colonial para and the Legion officers, who were more at home in the prevailing circumstances. Although the dissenters' actions were specifically inspired by a lack of faith in the commander's ability to bring about a victory, they were nevertheless symptomatic of growing disenchantment in the non-French sections of the French Army with the way the war was being run and the lack of support the Legion and colonial troops, bearing the brunt of the fighting, had received from France.

The problem was that, in the main, Indochina had been too far from western Europe to give rise to much interest there. It was a 'dirty' war and the professionals of

the Legion were left to get on with it. What interest there was seemed always to be negative: casualties were kept out of the French media for fear of left-wing protests; donors could refuse to allow their blood to be given to victims of the war; French conscripts were not to be deployed overseas, which ruled out their participation in Indochina; and in 1952, France broke up the German battalion, following criticism in the press. There were feelings of betrayal in the air.

The situation for the besieged French forces was desperate

The detached strongpoint 'Isabelle', and the perimeter posts 'Eliane' and 'Dominique' became the next targets for massed Viet Minh attacks on the night of 30 March. 'Isabelle', manned by a battalion of 3 REI plus colonial troops, refused to budge; 'Dominique' and 'Eliane' fell, but were later retaken, the latter by legionnaires of 2 REI. The French maintained their grip on the south and east of the fortress, but Giap's forces held the high ground to the north and northeast, and the creeping noose of Viet Minh trenches was getting tighter. The situation for the besieged French forces was desperate. France had already approached the USA for help and a number of options were considered and deemed either politically or militarily unviable, including, reportedly, the use of nuclear weapons.

The only way to deliver reinforcements now was by parachute

The only way to deliver reinforcements to Dien Bien Phu now was by parachute. From 10 April onwards, drops of paratroops from 2 BEP were made over the diminishing perimeter of the fortress. When the ranks of 2 BEP had been exhausted, volunteers from 3 REI and 5 REI stepped up who had never worn a parachute in their lives before. Dien Bien Phu was the 'hottest' DZ imaginable and many legionnaires did not reach the ground alive; of those that did many did not land in French-held areas; of those that landed in French-held areas, many died almost immediately in the fighting.

On 23 April legionnaires of 2 BEP tried to counter-

Opposite: A wounded and weary Legion lieutenant peers out of a sand-bagged position. The war in Indochina was to cost the Legion dearly in dead and wounded.

attack in the battle for strongpoint 'Huguette 1' with a bayonet charge; they were cut down by machine-gun fire. By the end of April, there was hardly anyone left to fight. Maimed and wounded legionnaires struggled back to their posts from the underground sick bay, often to return bearing even worse injuries.

When the Viet Minh assaulted on 6 May the strongpoint 'Eliane' was taken, the defenders making one last-ditch effort to break out of the Viet Minh ring surrounding them. Only 'Isabelle' and Tac HQ remained. A break out from Tac HQ was discussed but never happened and at 1730 on 7 May, the white flag appeared over Dien Bien Phu. Meanwhile, at 'Isabelle', five kilometres away, legionnaires of 3 REI hung on to the last. At midnight on 7/8 May, they poured out of the strongpoint towards the Viet Minh positions — only 12 got away. The siege was over after 57 days and with it ended France's Indochina campaign.

The defence of Dien Bien Phu cost the French dear in lives lost

The defence of Dien Bien Phu cost the French dear in lives lost. Of the 22,000 French troops killed in Indochina, over 4000 died at Dien Bien Phu alone. Of the 10,482 legionnaires killed in Indochina, over 1500 died at Dien Bien Phu. Of the 6328 legionnaires taken prisoner in the Indochina campaign, of whom only 2567 came back alive, 4000 were taken prisoner at Dien Bien Phu. In all, seven Legion battalions had ceased to exist.

Yet the men on the ground — not only the Legion, but the French troops and the colonial troops — fought with tenacity and courage against a numerically superior enemy with 200 artillery pieces. Giap committed 50,000 troops to Dien Bien Phu and at the end of the battle, 22,000 were dead or wounded.

But the cost to France and to the Legion of the Indochina campaign could not be measured in figures alone. Rumblings of disillusionment were audible within the ranks of the Legion and the colonial forces with the nation whose 'dirty' war they had been sent to fight. Those legionnaires who survived Indochina would not forget the comrades who had fallen at Dien Bien Phu and other battles. Nor would they forget that once again France had given them less than wholehearted support in their task. Over the next few years, these rumblings of discontent would grow steadily louder, to reach a climax in yet another colonial war, this time in Algeria.

ALGERIA: IN THE CRUCIBLE

The defeat at Dien Bien Phu brought the Legion back to their home in Algeria — only to face a colonial war that nearly resulted in the death of the *Légion Etrangère*.

On 8 May 1954, news of the French defeat at Dien Bien Phu reached the Legion garrison at Sidi-bel-Abbès, Algeria. The commander, Colonel Paul Gardy, organised a solemn ceremony of remembrance. Standing next to the old war memorial in front of the ranked legionnaires lining the great parade square, Gardy spoke in the silence following the buglers' mournful rendition of 'aux morts'. In a voice choked with emotion he read out the orders of the day.

'We are gathered to commemorate the heroic sacrifice of those who fell during that heroic struggle.

We are going to present arms to the banners of those units that disappeared in the battle....'

Colonel Gardy went on to read through the list of units lost at Dien Bien Phu, while his men paid their silent tribute. To the battalions of 13 DBLE, to the battalions of 2 and 3 REI, to 1 and 2 BEP, to the mortar companies of 3 and 5 REI, and to the many volunteers raised ad hoc and parachuted in during the final days of the battle.

Operation Kasbah, January 1957. This large-scale cordon and search operation in Algiers, conducted by paras, led to the dicovery of numerous FLN arms caches.

A Legion outpost on the Morice Line, an electrified fence running along the Algerian-Moroccan border, which proved highly effective in keeping FLN guerrillas out of Algeria.

Like those who fell at Camerone in 1863, the dead legionnaires of Dien Bien Phu would be long remembered.

After the debacle of Dien Bien Phu and the withdrawal of French Forces from Indochina the Legion returned home. But what exactly was home for the legionnaire? Certainly not mainland France, although this was the homeland of many individual legionnaires and the birthplace of the majority of Legion officers. Although the Legion had spent a total of 71 years in south east Asia the traditional home of the Legion, and the area in which most of its campaigns had been fought was, in fact, North Africa.

Algeria had been conquered by France after a campaign which had begun in 1830. The following occupation had resulted in almost a million French and other European nationals settling in the country. The situation in Algeria itself remained settled until after World War

Two, when the first demands for autonomy began to be voiced. In 1951 the main nationalist organisation, the *Front de Libération Nationale* (FLN), was established by Algerians seeking independence from France. Over the next few years it was to win increasing support both within and outside the country.

The legionnaires and the paras were to bear the brunt of the brutal war

However, the call for independence ran contrary to the long-held French belief that Algeria was an integral part of France, and it went largely unheeded by the colonial administration. The first major confrontation between nationalists and the security forces had taken place as early as 1948. Since that time there had been a series of low-level and random attacks on resident Europeans, but it was not until 1954 that the FLN embarked on a full-scale guerrilla war. The French responded by reinforcing their garrisons, and eventually increased the size of the army in Algeria to 450,000 men, including some 20,000

legionnaires and French Army paras. As in French Indochina, these two elite formations were to bear the brunt of the brutal war which was to follow. Unlike the war in Indochina, however, in Algeria it was not only the local population who were to resist French authority. 'The war for nothing', as it was judged by many in France, provoked a unique reaction among a number of these elite units. Those fighting the rebels were finally themselves to rebel, and the history of how this happened is both tragic and complex.

The shots fired on these defenceless civilians sparked the Algerian War

The immediate origins of the Algerian War (1954-62) lie perhaps in the French response to the civil disturbances which took place at the small Algerian market town of Setif in 1945. Local public celebrations in support of V-E Day gave way to demonstrations in favour of nationalism. The police over-reacted, shots were fired and several demonstrators killed. The level of violence escalated until

Legionnaires erect a searchlight on the Morice Line. Despite minefields and Legion patrols the FLN regularly attempted crossing the Line, often at heavy cost.

stopped by a combined operation involving a naval artillery bombardment and ground assault, supported by an accompanying aerial attack. The total European dead numbered 104 while the lowest estimate of the death toll among the Algerians was 1500. The seeds of Algerian insurrection were sown at Setif in May 1945, only to appear many miles away nine years later.

On 1 November 1954, the tentative calm of the Algerian situation was finally shattered. High in the Aurès mountains, on a winding and windswept road, a young French civilian and an ageing Arab employee of the French administration were brutally slain. M. Guy Monnerot, a teacher, together with his wife, and Hadj Sadok, a *caid* (locally appointed official), were travelling on a public bus when it was stopped by armed tribesmen. What actually occurred during the following incident is unclear, but the end result is certain: two civilians

were murdered, the *caid* killed outright, the teacher dying of his injuries before help arrived. Madame Monnerot was wounded by the burst of machine gun fire which left her husband mortally wounded, but she survived the attack. No-one on the bus had been armed.

The Legion's veteran units were withheld from the fray until mid-1955

The shots fired on these defenceless civilians began the Algerian War in earnest. Although a number of guerrilla attacks on military and police targets were carried out that day, it is the murder of M.Monnerot that is remembered as the spark that set Algeria ablaze. The fall of Dien Bien Phu convinced the FLN and the organisation's military arm — the *Armée de Libération Nationale* (ALN), that the French were not invincible. Algeria, or so thought nationalist leaders such as Ferhal Abbes, Klim Belkacem and Ben Bella, would achieve independence after a relatively short armed struggle. They were indeed to achieve their aims, but it was to take longer than they anticipated.

The French, initially reluctant to deploy their war-weary legionnaires following their return from Indochina,

Some of the 4400 suspects rounded up in a single operation in Algiers in 1956. The Legion was heavily involved in such unpopular urban policing tasks.

attempted to control the situation using local garrison troops. These men, the majority of whom were conscript soldiers, were not the battle-hardened veterans who would later play a vital role in the forthcoming combat. In the early stages of the conflict the Legion element in Algeria consisted solely of the training establishment at Sidi-bel-Abbès. The Legion's veteran units were withheld from the fray until mid-1955, and when they finally arrived in Algeria, found themselves confined to barracks on the grounds of an 'unspecified' epidemic. This reluctance to deploy them did not go down well with the legionnaires themselves, and the men were eager to get to grips with the enemy.

From the early days of their operational deployment to Algeria the Legion units faced a difficult task. For them it

The remains of FLN leader Ali La Pointe's hideout. Despite repeated requests, La Pointe refused to surrender, leaving the Legion no option but to use explosives to break in.

was *un boulot de flic* — a cop's job rather than a real campaign. The *fellagha,* as the enemy was known, were elusive, well-equipped and trained, and most important, were backed by the neighbouring Arab states of Egypt and Tunisia. In the early stages of the war the guerrillas restricted their activities to hit-and-run attacks on local government and security forces installations. They also attacked small patrols and dominated the surrounding areas through a process of intimidation and terror. In response to these attacks the Legion and para units mounted search-and-destroy missions. While these were often effective in catching the *fellagha* off guard they did not sufficiently inhibit their movement. In the early stages of the war the French had sufficient men to garrison towns and cities only, ceding large areas of the country to the enemy, who moved their men with comparative ease.

In 1956, the FLN changed tack and began an urban terror campaign

In 1956, however, due to improved French tactics, the FLN changed tack and began an urban terror campaign. This in turn led to bloody reprisals by the local European settler population, the *Pieds Noirs*, and, in some cases, by the local gendarmerie. As in the ALN's campaign, those suspected of allegiance to the French authorities were brutally beaten or butchered, often in front of their families and the local population. The French administration's reaction was more subtle, but no less deadly. Stories of police and army atrocities and torture abounded and, despite the passage of time and legal amnesty, continue to make the headlines in French newspapers some 30 years later.

With the urban campaign failing to make any real impression the FLN once again changed course and aimed for an all-out general strike, set for late January 1956. It was to be a massive civil protest of a passive nature, the like of which had never been seen before in Africa. To counter this proposed act of civil disobedience the French government ordered 10e Division Parachutistes (10 DP) into Algiers. Under the command of General Jacques Massu the force, which included the Legion's 1 REP, was tasked with restoring order 'using every possible means'. In keeping with the style of many such instructions giving the military carte blanche when dealing with 'civil disturbance', these orders were delivered verbally. Two days prior to the strike's deadline the ALN detonated three explosive devices in the busy shop-

ping area in the centre of the town. Twenty civilians were torn apart by the blasts and many others, small children among them, were mutilated for life. Despite this ruthless act perpetrated by the FLN the strike began as planned, only to be countered by the most successful strike-breaking operation in military history.

The Battle for Algiers had only just begun, at least for the men of 1 REP

Businesses were forcibly reopened if the proprietor refused to do so voluntarily. Owners who tried to escape were sought out and returned to their shops, and those who could not be found had their premises opened for them by legionnaires and paratroops. They returned later to find them devoid of stock, presumably lifted by passing trade during their absence. The public transport system was put back on the road, children were bused into school where, with a legionnaire or a para in attendance, they were taught by their reluctant teachers.

After three days of enforced activity the would-be strikers gave up and the population of Algiers drifted back to work. The general strike was a failure. However, the Battle for Algiers had only just begun, at least for the men of 1 REP. They had no illusions about the war in Algeria. Led by the dynamic and charismatic Colonel Pierre Jeanpierre, an experienced and distinguished officer who had witnessed the demise of 1 BEP, 1 REP were a hand-picked elite. Jeanpierre had chosen his men well. Among his officers was a former comrade-in-arms from Indochina, Capitaine Roger Faulques, and newer, younger subalterns such as Lieutenants Philippe Durand-Ruel,Philippe Erulin and Roger Degueldre — junior officers soon to prove themselves on the field of battle. In addition, Colonel Jeanpierre had an exceptionally strong cadre of senior *sous-officiers* led by his gifted Adjutant, Laszlo Tasnady. He turned the 1 REP into the Legion's *corps d'élite*, lean and mean — and ready for action.

1 REP was tasked with rooting out the subversives in the old Arab quarter

During the Battle for Algiers in 1957, 1 REP was tasked with rooting out the subversive element hidden within the old Arab quarter of the town. After six months of bitter fighting in the Aurès, the Nementcha, the Ouarsenis, and the Kabylie mountains, 1 REP had succeeded in destroying every major ALN group in their tactical area of operations. The enemy had now left the countryside for the town, and 1 REP followed. Working their way through the narrow streets of the warren-like Kasbah, the legionnaires ferreted out the urban *fellagha*. It took time, but the men of 1 REP remained firm to their purpose. The bombings and atrocities continued without respite as the hunt for the local ALN leaders carried on.

A third senior ALN commander, Ali la Pointe, was discovered

Among the first commander they captured was Larbi Ben M'Hidi, one of the six founder members of the ALN. In September the Legion paras swooped again, this time trapping another important leader, Yacef Sa'adi. Cornered by a 1 REP patrol led by the indomitable Jeanpierre, Sa'adi put up a spirited resistance before finally hurling a grenade from his hiding place. The resulting explosion injured the Colonel, who was recovered and evacuated by the ever-reliable Tasnady. The Legion tradition of leading from the front cost Jeanpierre a number of unwanted

grenade fragments and a month in hospital. Yacef Sa'adi demanded to be allowed to surrender to the civil authority, an honour he was graciously granted by the legionnaires. By the time the Colonel had been discharged fit from hospital Sa'adi was consorting with the French administration, and expounding the virtues of the FLN to the world press. It is not difficult to see why the Legion and Paratroop units began to draw the conclusion they were being let down, even betrayed, by their political masters.

Two weeks later, a third senior ALN commander, Ali la Pointe, was discovered hiding with other members of his cell in a concealed chamber behind the false wall of a Kasbah, at No.5 rue des Abdermanes. Despite calls for his surrender la Pointe refused to admit defeat and remained in hiding. This was one man 1 REP were not going to give up. They surrounded the building and began to lay

The FLN call for a general strike in January 1957 was widely supported, but Legion troops and French Paras broke the strike by forcing shopkeepers to reopen their premises.

The Algerian coup of 1961, supported by key units in the Legion, collapsed almost immediately in the face of public protest in mainland France.

explosive charges against the adjoining wall. After the fuse had been ignited a final call for his surrender was given by the OIC firing party. The reply, la Pointe's last verbal testimonial, was 'Merde!' Apparently, the legionnaires laid their charges directly opposite la Pointe's own cache and, perhaps luckily for the Legion but unfortunately for the ALN leader, the resulting detonation brought the house down. It took several more days to recover the bodies of Ali la Pointe and 16 of his colleagues. From then on the situation in the Kasbah area of Algiers was decidedly quieter.

By late 1957, 1 REP had pioneered the techniques of airmobile warfare and were constantly deployed by helicopter into areas known to contain ALN groups. They were the French Army's quick reaction unit and dealt with the guerrillas who broke through the barricaded borders and infiltrated into Algeria. New tactics were evolved to deal with the threat that remained after the Moroccan and Tunisian borders were sealed by electrified fences. The fence along the Tunisian frontier was known as the 'Guelma Line' and that along the Moroccan border as the 'Morice Line'. They were built one mile

inside the frontiers with blockhouses constructed at regular intervals. The 'no-man's-land' was mined and subject to regular patrols.

On Camerone Day 1958, a well-armed ALN band was located between the border and Duvivier. The first company sent to deal with the guerrillas was pinned down by heavy and accurate machine-gun fire. A second company was helicoptered in and advanced line abreast towards the enemy positions. It looked like a battle from the 18th Century, but with a difference; on command, the line dropped into cover and, on a given signal, each man threw one grenade. Then they advanced another 100m and repeated the action. Using this new technique, Jeanpierre found his men were able to clear the hills and valleys with the minimum of casualties to themselves, and with devastating effect on the enemy. On that day alone the two 1 REP companies killed 192 rebels, captured five ALN guerrillas and recovered a large quantity of modern weapons. 1 REP had their own rules for combat: act only on accurate and precise information; employ fighter ground-attack aircraft to support assaults whenever possible; do not rely solely on artillery fire; attack at first light and consolidate before dusk; strip equipment down to the bare essentials and fight light; and, above all, be aggressive and keep moving. Under the direction of Colonel Jeanpierre 1 REP achieved considerable success, but their victories were not without a price.

On 29 May 1958, two guerrilla groups were located in high ground close to 'Guelma'. Two companies of Legion paras were inserted by helicopter and were immediately engaged by the enemy. From well-sited defensive positions in the cliffs the *fellagha* poured down a hail of fire on to the legionnaires stuck in the tangled web of undergrowth below. Air-to-ground attack and artillery fire failed to make any real impression on the defenders, and

French Army tanks rumble through central Paris in April 1961 to defend the capital against the threat from rebellious elements of the Armed Forces.

the attack ground to a halt. At midday, Jeanpierre's small Alouette helicopter skimmed over the low scrub covering the legionnaires' positions on Mermera Hill.

It was a risk, but one that the Colonel had taken many times before

It was a common enough sight for the paras; Jeanpierre crouched over a map, wearing a headset on top of his green Legion beret and directing the battle from above. Searching out a clear way forward for his troops, Jeanpierre ordered his pilot to make a second pass over the enemy positions.

It was a risk, but one that the Colonel had taken many times before. Today would prove the last time. As the Alouette crested the ridge a second time it was hit by accurate ground fire from the *fellagha* hiding in the caves. As one round severed the fuel line, the engine spluttered and died. Too low to auto-gyrate, the pilot had little chance to recover and the aircraft ploughed nose-first into the bushes. A rifle section raced across to the

broken helicopter and dragged out their unconscious commander and his pilot. There was little that they could do, however, and Colonel Pierre Jeanpierre died as his men, saddened and enraged by his death, successfully stormed the crest.

'Rather die, *mon colonel*, than leave Algeria in the hands of the FLN'

Jeanpierre's death was a blow to both 1 REP and the Legion. He had served in Syria, Indochina and Suez — a total of 25 years. More than 30,000 people attended his funeral, where Salan and his generals paid tribute to one of France's most decorated and respected officers. His own men and officers felt the loss more keenly than most, and Lieutenant Roger Degueldre swore an oath over his commander's coffin — one which was both prophetic and would influence the events that were to follow: 'Rather die, *mon colonel*, than leave Algeria in the hands of the FLN.' The Legion was soon to leave Algeria, but many of its members would remain, either as corpses or as members of the OAS — the *Organisation de l'Armée Secrète*.

By 1958, the French Army, and the Legion in particular, needed governmental reassurance. Throughout the Legion's campaign in Algeria France's political administration had been particularly unstable. Since 1954 there had been six different governments and it was not until de Gaulle took office as Prime Minister in June 1958 that the Army felt they had a political leader on whom they could rely. Three days after his appointment, de Gaulle visited Algeria, spoke with the military commanders and visited Jeanpierre's tomb. He offered reassurance and left the distinct impression that he would not abandon Algeria to the FLN.

The year 1959 was an active one for the Legion. 1 REP accounted for 972 rebels with losses of only 42 legionnaires killed and 97 wounded. The 3 REI figures included 462 guerrillas killed and 664 taken prisoner, while 2 REC killed some 383 *fellagha* — impressive statistics, but costly. Legion fatal casualties in the Algerian campaign amounted to more than 2000. But they were winning.

'The OAS strikes where it wishes' claims this wall cartoon showing a club poised over the head of General De Gaulle. OAS members were drawn largely from the Legion and Paras.

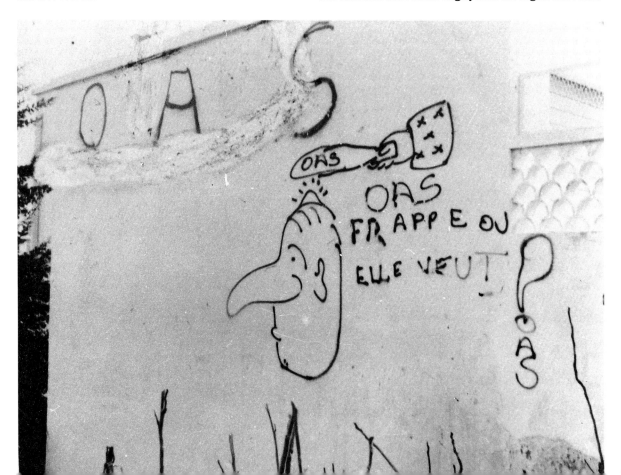

Together with France's paratroops, the legionnaires distinguished themselves on the field of battle in Algeria. Despite their success, French governments, including de Gaulle's from 1958, had to reconcile themselves to the fact that a political solution to the war would have to be found. In the post-colonial world the wishes and aspirations of the Algerians would have to be taken into account, and this would mean talking to the FLN. This would be interpreted as a sell-out, especially by the many legionnaires who had won hard-earned victories in Algiers and elsewhere in the country. These men, who lived, fought and occasionally died for France, saw themselves being let down by the political administration of their adopted country. They were dying for a lost cause.

The ALN's combat strength was reduced from over 100,000 to 15,000

General Maurice Challe had replaced Salan as commander-in-chief of Algeria in late 1958. Challe was a brilliant strategist, tactician and leader of men who completely reorganised France's war effort to remarkable effect. Within months, the ALN's combat strength was reduced from over 100,000 to 15,000, and the liberation movement

was effectively stopped in its tracks. The FLN was only kept alive by the fact they were located outside the country in Tunisia. Then, in January 1960, disaster struck. De Gaulle sacked General Massu, the popular leader of the 10th Parachute Brigade. Massu had criticised de Gaulle in a newspaper article over a broadcast the President had made in the previous September which had hinted at Algerian independence. Massu's sacking was interpreted by the European population as a concession to the FLN. They began to demonstrate and direct confrontations with the local Gendarmerie took place — resulting in a number of civilian casualties. The regular French Army units refused to move against the colons and it was only after the 10th Para Brigade, including 1 REP, was deployed to the troubled areas that calm was restored.

A full-scale and bloody civil war had been narrowly averted but the situation was not wholly resolved. Over the following year the government made further concessions to the FLN and a number of officers resigned their commissions in protest. Others prepared to rebel. Salan,

Edmond Jouhaud, André Zeller, Paul Gardy (Inspector of the Legion) and Challe formed the OAS in January 1961. De Gaulle, aware of the plot against him but uninformed as to its precise nature, had recalled Dufour, the CO of 1 REP a year earlier. He was replaced by Colonel Guiraud. During the summer of 1960, de Gaulle held talks with FLN leaders and in November during a radio broadcast had talked of an independent Algeria.

Convinced de Gaulle would betray the army, the generals prepared a coup

Convinced the President would betray the army, the generals prepared a coup d'état. The plotters chance came when Guiraud, a staunch Gaullist, took leave and passed command to Commandant Elie Saint Marc. Salan was in Spain, and Challe and Zeller moved back to Algeria. Challe recruited Saint Marc, without whose co-operation 1 REP would have played no real role in the events that followed, and early on 22 April 1961, the rebel forces moved into action. 1 REP took over key government installations and captured four leading generals opposed to the revolt. Within an hour they held the local police stations and government offices, but they had overlooked one vital aspect of any coup — outside communications. The telephone lines to Paris remained intact and, as a consequence of this oversight, troops in France were activated and put on standby to move to Algeria. In mainland France public opinion was strongly against the coup, but to the French in Algiers the rebel legionnaires were heroes.

However, not all Legion units came out in support of the coup. 2 REP support for their comrades was dampened by their commander, Colonel Darmuzai, who kept his troops static although agreeing to the revolt in principle. 1 REC was even less forthcoming. Its officers took the side of the rebels, but rather than physically support them deployed to the hills in search of the FLN. The commander of 13 DBLE, Colonel Vaillant, was not a rebel supporter, a fact that he clearly demonstrated to those under his command. Parading his entire officer and *sous-officier* cadre he stated simply: 'If you wish to join this seditious uprising, gentlemen, there is a preliminary step. You will have to get rid of your commanding officer.'

13 DBLE continued its operations against the *fellagha* in the Kabylie mountains. Other Legion senior officers, including Colonel Brothier at Sidi-bel-Abbès, were unable to agree to the involvement of the Legion in politics. He

and his command stayed put. This division between Legion elements was further exacerbated by by the fact that Salan and Challe were in disagreement over what to do next. Challe and his colleagues had no political aspirations — they were purely military men. Salan, on the other hand, was more politically motivated and an important member of the OAS. With the two men advocating different approaches the rebel movement was hopelessly divided. More important than these internal divisions, however, was the fact that the French Army, Navy and Air Force were overwhelmingly opposed to the action.

The rebellion had begun on a Saturday and by Tuesday it was over

The rebellion had begun on a Saturday and by Tuesday it was over. Had the Legion units in Algeria teamed up from the beginning the uprising might have stood a better chance of success. Even today there are still those who are adamant that the plan could have succeeded. Among the legionnaires there was talk of dropping paratroops on to Paris itself, although the transport aircraft would probably have been shot down by Air Force fighters. Nevertheless, the men would have jumped. But it was not to be. By first light on Wednesday 1 REP had returned to their base and Saint Marc informed his regiment that it was to be disbanded and dispersed. For the time being at least he remained in command, but two gendarmes accompanied him everywhere.

The angry and disillusioned legionnaires vacated their camp

On 27 April, the angry and disillusioned legionnaires vacated their camp, first destroying their barracks and burning everything that could not be transported to Sidi-bel-Abbès and Saidi. Many did not arrive at their destinations, preferring to desert en route to join the OAS. Of the Legion's 650 officers 200 had by now been arrested and taken into custody. Camerone Day passed without ceremony. Bastille Day followed. On 14 July, France's most decorated military formation went unrepresented at the parade, and their battle flags remained unseen by the celebrants. The *Légion Etrangère* was in disgrace.

Legion HQ at Sidi-bel-Abbès, Algeria, in 1962. After dismantling the *Monument aux Morts*, 1 RE left Sidi on 13 November 1962 for their new home in France.

READY FOR ANYTHING

The Legion survived the fierce combat and equally fierce internal strife of two World Wars, Indochina and Algeria to emerge in the 1960s as a crucial element in France's *Force d'Action Rapide*, ready to deploy anywhere in the the world that French interests were felt to be at risk. And there was no shortage of action: in Kolwezi, Chad and in Lebanon, as part of the UN peacekeeping force, the modern Legion has proved itself to be ready for anything.

In the years immediately after Algerian independence and the French withdrawal the future of the *Légion Etrangère* looked very bleak. France seriously debated whether she still needed her Legion. It was a debate eventually won by the Legion and its supporters, but it was a close run thing. For the first time in its history the Legion had units based in metropolitan France. Its overseas commitments and, consequently, its raison d'être, seemed to be waning. Or were they? France had pulled out of Indochina

Commando training in French Guyana often involves instruction in the use of unusual weapons. The crossbow can be a lethal device, ideal when a silent kill is crucial.

119

These former legionnaires have earned the right to live at the Legion's Puyloubier rest home by serving for at least 20 years — four five-year contracts.

and Algeria after long and highly damaging campaigns to remain in control, but the country still had numerous interests abroad. Many developing nations, former French colonies and protectorates, still had close links with their recent administrators and France provided these new governments with financial aid and physical support. Countries such as Chad, Djibouti and the Central African Republic depended heavily on French assistance. Ultimately, the French government was probably unwilling to disband a unit which could be used to fight unpopular wars and which on many occasions had proved itself more than willing to shed blood for France. In World War One, for example, the Legion's contribution to the Allied victory can be measured in terms of the sacrifices made: the Legion lost some 31,000 dead, missing and wounded in major Allied offensives along the Western Front.

The battles of Vimy Ridge, the Marne, the Somme and the Bois de Hangard are woven into the battle honours of many a Legion regiment. During the Somme offensive alone the Legion's *Régiment de Marche* lost one in every three men. More than 44,000 foreigners of over 100 dif-

ferent nationalities fought with the Legion during the four years of war. Austro-Hungarians, Turks and Germans fought alongside Belgians and Americans, all united under the flags of France and the French Foreign Legion. Despite their country being at war with France, the German legionnaires, always considered among the best troops serving in the Legion, remained loyal to their adopted 'motherland' and fought alongside their colleagues. In fact, France's most decorated *sous-officier* of the war was *Sergent-chef* Mader, a German legionnaire.

At the end of World War One, France still occupied, or at least protected, many colonies and countries around the world. One of the more important of these protectorates was Morocco, with 322,000 square miles of largely inhospitable terrain which needed to be policed by France. This country's conquest and pacification had been made possible largely through the efforts of the

Legion. In the years between the two World Wars the Legion was kept busy in keeping the peace, manning the forts, putting down rebellions and building roads. Like their Roman counterparts of 2000 years ago, the construction of roads has been a traditional task of legionnaires and, when Morocco gained independence in 1939, it could boast one of the finest road systems in northern Africa, largely the fruit of nearly 40 years of Legion toil.

A single Legion battalion was attacked by an enemy force of 3000 tribesmen

While French forces were heavily involved with controlling Morocco, Legion detachments were busy countering attempts made by Muslim nationalists to gain control of Syria and the Lebanon. Inspired by the initial successes of the Moroccan nationalist leader, Abd el-Krim, the Syrian Druze tribesmen and the newly-formed Peoples' Party mounted a jihad or 'holy war' against the French. The campaign began in 1925 and at first the rebels achieved considerable success. But within 18 months the Legion, supported by aircraft and armour, broke the disorganised

Druze resistance and restored the peace. The Druze, though ill-equipped to fight a modern war and relying on superior numbers attacking en masse, were a constant threat to smaller Legion detachments.

In one instance, in September 1925, the insignificant town of Messifre, defended by a single Legion battalion, was attacked by an enemy force numbering over 3000 tribesmen. In the two-day battle to gain control of Messifre, the Syrians lost 1000 dead or wounded to Legion bullet and bayonet, while the defenders suffered only 47 killed and 83 wounded. Despite these heavy losses the Druze attacks almost overwhelmed the legionnaires, who were saved only by the timely arrival of French ground-attack aircraft. At Rachaya, in November, a squadron from 1 REC held off 3000 tribesmen for four days. The arrival of a relief column prevented Rachaya from becoming a second Camerone.

The situation in Syria was finally brought under con-

Legionnaires sprint forward under fire during the Legion's spirited break-out through the encircling Axis forces at Bir Hakeim, north Africa, in June 1942.

trol in 1927 after the French High Command adopted the policy of bombing those towns and villages which were sympathetic to the rebels. The Druze tribesmen escaped to the mountains and the Legion remained to police the area until their withdrawal, following the allied invasion of Syria, in 1941.

Units of the Legion distinguished themselves throughout World War Two

In the years immediately before World War Two, critics saw the Legion as a merely colonial formation, with a large percentage of German *sous-officiers* (suspected by some of having been infiltrated by German military intelligence). Others, however, realised the growing demand for experienced soldiers. Legion units fought against the German advance into France during the summer of 1940, while a Legion Task Force, originally tasked with support-

ing the Finns against the Russian invasion but prevented from gaining access to the Baltic because of a German blockade, succeeded in storming and capturing Narvik in Norway. Despite their success, the legionnaires had to relinquish their grip on the German stronghold and were reassigned to bolster the French divisions attempting to halt the German drive to the French Channel ports.

The Legion was too late, and indeed too small, to make any difference to the outcome. The French divisions collapsed, the government began to make moves toward surrender and those legionnaires who had survived the collapse, together with the defeated British and French troops, made their way across the Channel to England. The two battalions of 13 DBLE were addressed

A legionnaire of 13 DBLE raises the standard in Libya during the Allied campaign in north Africa. During World War Two other elements of the Legion fought for the Axis.

Singing is as important for the Legion's officers as it is for the rank and file. These officers belong to 4 RE at Castelnaudary, the Legion's training centre.

by General Charles de Gaulle, leader of the Free French forces in England. 'Who did the Legion wish to fight for, Vichy France or Free France?' Half, mostly Germans and Italians, came down on the side of the Vichy régime and were returned to Morocco to be disbanded. The others remained as 13 DBLE and were largely absorbed by the Anglo-American forces.

The Legion units that found themselves under Vichy control were starved of equipment and recruits. In North Africa, 1 REI remained at Sidi-bel-Abbès but 2 REI and 2 REC were disbanded while 1 REC was substantially reduced in strength. In Morocco, 3 REI remained on garrison duty, 4 REI became 4 DBLE and was despatched to Senegal in west Africa, while 6 REI formed part of the garrison in Syria.

13 DBLE returned to the desert, this time to Libya, where they played a vital role in the action at Bir Hakeim. Supporting the Allied line to the south of Tobruk against Rommel's spectacular offensive in May 1942 were two Legion battalions among a Free French force of 5500 troops. Under the command of General Koenig the

French Forces, comprised mostly of colonial troops, held out for 15 days against German and Italian armoured, artillery and air attacks. With little support from their Allies, with the notable exception of the Royal Air Force, the French were desperately short of ammunition and water when the orders came to pull back. However, their spirited defence had gained the Allies' forces time to regroup, and though their efforts went largely unnoticed by the public, their successful holding action was critical in the Allies' eventual victory in the Western Desert.

Other Legion units were integrated into US formations

Units of the Legion continued to distinguish themselves throughout the remainder of the war, especially during the Allied advance into Italy. By this time 13 DBLE was part of General Juin's Free French Corps within the British 8th Army. In August 1944, it took part in Operation Dragoon, the Allied invasion of Southern France. Other Legion units were integrated into US formations. So by the end of World War Two, while the Legion continued to survive, it had lost much of its original character. The old Legion of Morocco and Syria was gone forever.

After World War Two, the Legion was hurled into the

fight against the Viet Minh in Indochina. The Legion bore the brunt of this brutal and bitter campaign and by the war's end was almost an Army itself, totalling some 36,000 men. Ousted from south east Asia, France began to turn its attention to troubles closer to home, this time in Algeria. The final result was the same — France withdrew her troops and the Legion left another home.

'The legionnaire is an outlaw who has fallen out of the ranks of society'

The French Armed Forces contain a large percentage of conscripts undergoing their compulsory national service. In the case of France's army, *L'Armée de Terre,* the conscripts make up around 70% of the total force. The remainder are full-time professional soldiers, *sous-officiers* and officers who, for the most part, provide the national service element with its training and leadership cadre. This means that military formations, especially those at Regimental level, contain an especially high number of non-professional troops. French conscripts cannot be sent overseas without employing special governmental legislation.

The Legion therefore performs an invaluable function because France, while it may be willing to shed blood to retain influence abroad, prefers it not to be from the veins of a Frenchman, especially one who has not volunteered to die for his country. So it is that France's *Légion Etrangère* plays such a vital role in operations and deployments overseas. Any blood spilled will not be 'officially' French, and therefore will do little political damage. Legionnaires respond well to the task. As General Villebois-Mareuill said in 1912: 'The legionnaire is an outlaw who has fallen out of the ranks of orderly human society, where he was ill at ease. He has a natural taste for risks. He wants to live his life. It is the only personal property left to him and he stakes it boldly.'

Aware of the risks and willing to accept them, legionnaires had fought and died for France, both bravely and in great numbers. They'd earned the rights of Frenchmen; as the Legion poet Pascal Bonetti put it in 1914:

N'est pas cet étranger devenu fils de France

Non par le sang reçu mais par le sang versé ?

(Has not this foreigner become a son of France

Not through blood inherited but through blood spilled?)

The motto of the *Légion Etrangère* remained 'The Legion is Our Country'. The Legion needed France and, above all, France needed it. Protected from the political

axe by an admiring public and its own previous achievements, the Legion marched on.

In the period immediately after the Algerian War the Legion underwent intense restructuring and reorganisation. Its manpower was reduced from 20,000 to 8000. Many of the Legion's combat elements were transferred to Corsica while the Sidi-bel-Abbès establishment relocated to Aubagne near Marseilles. The majority of those in Corsica found it difficult to adjust, morale reached an all-time low and desertion increased.

There was even talk that the Legion might be 'sold off' to the United States

There was even talk that the Legion might be 'sold off' to the United States of America. However, despite its reduction in strength and the lowering in morale, the Legion was better off than many 'colonial' units. France's *Armée d'Afrique* was effectively dismantled and, between 1959 and 1964, 32 of its regiments were disbanded. Units with long traditions, such as the Tirailleur infantry, the Zouaves, the Spahis and the Chasseurs, were greatly changed, both for political and economic reasons.

It was not only the *Armée d'Afrique* that suffered. France's airborne forces were also among those hard hit by de Gaulle's purges after the Algerian putsch. The two elite Divisions Parachutistes, 10e DP (to which 1 REP belonged) and 25e DP (of which 2 REP was a part) were both disbanded. So too were individual regiments including 14e Para and 18e Para and the Air Force's para-commandos, the Fusiliers Commandos. In addition, the officer corps underwent extensive reorganisation and many of its members, including a number from the Legion, were imprisoned, purged or forced to retire. In many ways the Legion fared better than most.

The Legion could see light at the end of the tunnel

By the mid-1960s the situation had become calmer and the Legion had settled down to its new way of life. The low morale and misgivings about political treachery and interference within the Legion from those outside was replaced by a more stable attitude as new recruits, unaf-

Right: 'Watch and shoot' — a Legion anti-tank gunner prepares to engage a target. The LRAC-89 is the standard light anti-tank weapon of the French Army.

fected by recent history, joined the Corps. The Legion was beginning to see light at the end of the tunnel, especially when the planned overseas deployments came into effect. Small detachments were deployed in the Sahara in support of France's rapidly diminishing 'empire' but the real change came about when 13 DBLE was posted to Djibouti, formerly French Somaliland, and 3 REI was transferred to Diego Suarez in Madagascar.

Caillaud restructured the companies for specialist missions

In addition to these changes, Legion units became part of combined, all-arms formations with specific missions. This new policy meant that three of six Legion regiments were deployed to areas outside metropolitan France and Corsica, while the remainder were given responsibilities within France itself.

An insight into the new approach adopted by the Legion can be better gained by examining the changes undergone by 2 REP during the 1960s. In June 1963, 2 REP was taken over by a new commander, Lieutenant-

Colonel Caillaud, a tough, energetic and far-sighted officer who was not only to have a great influence on the regiment's future development, but the future specialist role of the Legion as a whole. Until his arrival 2 REP had been trained in the role of conventional paratroops (airborne infantry) and was organised purely for airborne assault missions. Caillaud began to train the *compagnies de combat* for the more specialised para-commando role, and restructured the companies for specialist missions such as sabotage, mountain and ski warfare, amphibious operations and long-range reconnaissance.

This was not an entirely original concept, as during World War Two there had been two French Special Air Service regiments operating under Allied command. However, the idea of dividing a regiment into specialist companies was a new one and the radical change represented a completely different type of role for both 2 REP and for its legionnaires. Selection criteria necessarily

Legionnaires in Guyana paddle down river in a native pirogue, made from a hollowed-out tree trunk. Such boats are often the only means of insertion in the area.

became more stringent and the training tougher and much more varied. The Legion's paras adopted the para-commando role with enthusiasm and the next two years were spent acquiring the necessary skills and techniques demanded by their new mission. Re-enlistment went up and the regiment acquired both a new image and a new home.

The Legion's parachutists were now classed as para-commandos

In June 1967, 2 REP moved into their present base at Calvi in Corsica. The island has over 1000km of coastline, and mountains which rise to over 2700m. Its diverse terrain provides provides 2 REP with an ideal area in which to conduct specialised training. In addition, there is a parachute drop zone conveniently located just on the border of Camp Raffalli, the regimental base.

Between 1969 and 1971, 2 REP again saw active service overseas. While its headquarters and support elements remained in Corsica, its *compagnies de combat* rotated through operational deployments in Chad. This developing nation, a former French territory, had signed a security agreement with its former colonial masters, and in Spring 1969 the first Legion paras were sent to support its government.

Throughout 1973 the Legion adapted to its new role. 2 REP, the Legion's sole surviving parachute regiment, came under the command of 11e Division de Parachutistes (11 DP), a formation based in mainland France. Initially organised and equipped as a standard French Army parachute regiment, 2 REP now found itself providing the Division's vanguard element. The Legion's parachutists were now classed as 'para-commandos' rather than 'airborne infantry,' and each of the four *compagnies de combat* had its own specialist role, making them well suited for spearheading any airborne assault.

The Legion's three armoured reconnaissance squadrons, which belong to 1 REC, were also stationed in metropolitan France, but this time on the mainland.

The control room at the French space centre at Kourou in the Pacific. The installation is guarded by the Legion, as is the French nuclear test site on the atoll of Mururoa.

Tasked with the protection of vital points and strategic installations against the Spetsnaz-type threat in the event of mobilisation, 1 REC also began to provide detachments for operational tours overseas. This practise of rotating companies and squadrons through 'active service' postings abroad is one that has continued up to the present day. In the early 1970s, when the new policy was implemented, it was the Legion's raison d'être. In 1973 one regiment was in Madagascar and the nearby Comoro Islands; a second had its base in New Caledonia, supporting the French Pacific nuclear test site, with an element on the island of Tahiti, while a third regiment took up station in French Somaliland at the southern end of the Red Sea. Each of these locations was vital to France both from a strategic and a political point of view. They were equally important to the Legion, as these assignments showed that it was, if not exactly in favour with the government, at least trusted enough to carry out responsible tasks.

By the mid-1970s, the Legion was truly adept in its

A French para searching for anti-personnel mines. The men of *11e Division Parachutiste* maintain a healthy rivalry with the Legion's own paras of 2 REP.

A Legion patrol pauses during a routine sweep through sparsely vegetated bushland. The wide-brimmed sunhats shown here are no longer standard Legion issue.

many and varied roles but had had little chance to prove itself. However, this situation was soon to change and in February 1976 a Legion detachment became involved in a now largely forgotten incident in Djibouti. While on a routine training mission, the *2e compagnie* of 2 REP participated in the rescue of a number of children held hostage at Loyada. A school bus carrying 29 French children was captured by anti-government rebels on the border of Djibouti and Somalia. Four of the five rebels and, sadly, two children, were killed in the dramatic rescue.

The bus was situated right on the border, only yards from the Somalian border check-point at Loyada. Its precise location was no accident, as the rebels reckoned on France not risking a possible border incident with a 'friendly' neighbour, while it also provided them with an avenue of escape should French forces attempt a rescue. In the event this 'avenue' was effectively denied them by a wall of fire put down by armoured cars of 1 REC. As the *2e compagnie* assaulted the bus, snipers from the

A Legion desert patrol in Chad. The goggles and scarves these men wear protect them from the sun and sand. In the background is a 4x4 VLRA cross-country vehicle.

Gendarmerie counter-terrorist group, GIGN, picked off the children's captors, while legionnaires from 13 DBLE's nearby detachment acted as cut-offs, preventing escape or outside intervention. The operation was a great success and many lives were saved. Two years later 2 REP became involved in another rescue mission, but on a far larger scale. The dramatic operation in Kolwezi (examined in detail in the next chapter), gave the Legion the opportunity to show the French military, and indeed the world, just what its capabilities were.

France provided a military assistance package of 2000 troops

If 1978 could be considered special by the legionnaires themselves it would probably be because that year marked the Legion's return to Chad. The country had lost its first president, M.Tombalbaye, in April 1975. This had proved a blow not only to the developing nation but also to its former rulers, who had made every effort to secure close links with the President. His replacement, General Felix Malloum, arranged a short-lived peace with a leader of the dissident group responsible for the assassination of

his predecessor, Paris-educated Hissen Habré. The ceasefire lasted just days and the government was quick to turn to France for help.

France's immediate response was to provide a military assistance package of some 2000 troops, including an armoured cavalry squadron belonging to 1 REC, and one compagnie from 2 REI, a combined total of some 300 legionnaires. Over the next 18 months Legion detachments were to rotate through the country on four-month tours. These operational tours were relatively short by Legion standards, partly due to the high local sickness rate, and because the Legion wanted as many of its men as possible to experience this operational environment.

Chad was, and indeed still is, considered an operational posting. Conditions are harsh and tropical disease endemic, and hepatitis A and B also creates minor havoc among members of the Legion. Political unrest and the grand designs of Chad's northern neighbour, Libya, have also been a continual problem. In 1978 the two northern nationalist movements, one led by Habré, the other by General Goukouni Ouedeye, joined forces against the southern-dominated government forces. Libya's President, Colonel Gaddafi, offered his support to the northern factions.

Djedda was recaptured after a two day battle, at the cost of one Jaguar jet

In April 1978 the first French unit supporting the government forces saw action in the conflict. In the town of Salal, some 250 miles to the north of the capital, an armoured car of 1 REC engaged and destroyed a Soviet-built BTR armoured personnel carrier belonging to rebel forces who had taken up residence. The town was eventually re-occupied by government troops, but not until the French patrol had laid down a barrage of 90mm rounds from their vehicle-mounted cannon.

As instructors or as supporting sections the legionnaires were involved in continual skirmishes with the rebels. A month after the incident at Salal a training team belonging to 2 REP joined forces with a 1 REC patrol in an attempt to retake the town of Ati, which had been occupied by the rebels. After a mad, midnight drive across the desert only two armoured vehicles arrived at the rendezvous, but nevertheless the paratroops went in. During the next few days the same Legion group attacked the neighbouring town of Djedda, supported by fighter aircraft. Djedda was recaptured after a two day battle, at the cost of one Jaguar jet, downed by a rebel SAM-7. France was becoming increasingly committed.

The Chadean armed forces continued fighting but neither their efforts, nor those of President Giscard D'Estaing's government, could stay the general anti-administration feeling. In March 1979 General Malloum went into self-imposed exile in Nigera and by September that year Goukouni had taken up the reigns of power and was established in the country's capital. Habré had been

FIBUA training plays an important part in the modern Legion's programme. This legionnaire's FA-MAS is fitted with a blank firing attachment on the muzzle.

sentenced to death and was in exile. The final remnants of France's second intervention force were withdrawn by May 1980, nine months before Libyan President Gaddafi declared Libya and Chad to be one country.

The Legion prevented Gaddafi from overrunning his poorer neighbour

In Operation Manta in Chad in 1984, the Legion prevented Gaddafi from overrunning his poorer neighbour. Ordered by the Chadean head-of-state, General Goukouni, to leave the country in 1981, Libyan advisors and technicians had sabotaged installations and facilities before going — which had fuelled ill-feeling between the two countries. Although Goukouni had been prompted to take this action by France's President Mitterand, Chad's leader soon found himself alone and fighting a short civil war against his former ally Hissen Habré. Habré ousted Goukouni in June 1982, who then turned to Gaddafi for help. A guerrilla war began, with Goukouni's forces supported by Libyan regulars. At this point, French troops and aircraft were called in and deployed in support of Habré's government.

In January 1984, Libyan forces pushed south and captured the town of Ziguey, and a French Jaguar aircraft on a reconnaissance mission was shot down, killing the pilot. The French forces in Chad were bound by political restraints from taking firm action, and Libyan troops continued to advance into Chad. Gaddafi boasted 'we will inflict on France a defeat worse than Dien Bien Phu.' Despite this preposterous threat, a cease-fire was arranged. France and Libya withdrew their troops and a temporary government was established by Goukouni to the north of the 15th parallel.

Gaddafi, described by *The Economist* in December 1984 as 'a man from whom most other people would not buy a used promise', duly reneged on his cease-fire agreement. In February 1986, Libyan-backed rebels crossed into Chad-controlled territory. France flew in reinforcements, including elements of the Legion, and fierce fighting broke out, centred around the towns of Oum Chalouba and Ziguey. The Libyan push was eventually beaten back with the Libyans losing heavily in terms of men and war material. Chad remains the centre of

A French patrol in Chad. Bringing up the rear is a Panhard AML-60 armoured car mounted with a 60mm mortar and a 7.62mm co-axial machine gun.

attention and the Legion maintains a permanent presence in the county, with companies rotating through the country on training exercises. Any future conflict between the two countries would undoubtedly involve elements of the Legion in a major capacity.

The Legion maintains units in far flung corners of the globe

In 1982 the Legion undertook a different type of action, this time in the 'peacekeeping' role. It was a task which had previously been undertaken by the *Parachutistes d'Infanterie Marine* of France's *Force d'Action Rapide*, and one which was to mark a radical change in the usual policy of using elements of the Legion for an 'aggressive response', albeit in a defensive or supportive role. Today the Legion maintains units in far flung corners of the globe, and the traditional postings in France, Djibouti, Guyane and the Pacific atolls remain. Smaller legion formations, perhaps comprising only two or three companies, continue to deploy to countries with which France maintain close-links, on 'goodwill' and training missions. However, with the increase of large-scale international terrorism the opportunities for a legionnaire to take part in a 'peacekeeping' operation have steadily increased.

The Legion has had to adapt its tactics to changing circumstances

Both the legionnaires themselves, and their immediate superiors, are now expected to undertake missions requiring more 'diplomatic' skills, operations where keeping a cool head matters more than an immediate, instinctive response. These are missions where the need not to react violently to an apparent threat must be replaced by a more considered and less aggressive response. In the past, the Legion would have been considered too aggressive a unit for such jobs.

But nowadays the legionnaire, like so many of his colleagues in the western world's armies, is expected to think carefully before acting. Non-combatant casualties in 'civil-policing' style operations are unacceptable today, and the Legion has had to adapt its tactics accordingly. That they have done so, a fact borne out by the success of their peacekeeping mission to Beirut, illustrates not just the adaptability of the individual legionnaire, but of the Legion 'system' as well.

RESCUE AT KOLWEZI

When a bloody revolt broke out in Zaire in May 1978 thousands of European settlers were taken hostage by the rebels in the mining town of Kolwezi. As the situation in the town deteriorated, with the rebels running out of control, a wholesale massacre was feared. In the face of the Zairean Army's inability to control the situation, the Legion was called in. Within 24 hours of receiving the call to arms the paras of 2 REP had left their base in Corsica and were winging their way to Africa. There, despite a desperate lack of equipment, they pulled off a brilliant rescue operation.

The Legion's paratroopers had faced many dangerous missions since their birth in the Indochina war. From the jungles of Vietnam to the desert of Algeria, the paras had often fought hard battles against impossible odds. These actions were quickly forgotten by an ungrateful France. During the Algerian war, 1 REP had been disbanded, the paras left Africa in disgrace. The Legion in general, and 2 REP in particular, had worked hard to eradicate the suspicion that they were not to be trusted. During the month of May 1978, 2 REP was to prove to France and to the world that it was a thoroughly professional and elite unit

A Legion sniper, armed with an FRF rifle, takes aim from the bonnet of a commandeered commercial vehicle as the Legion sweeps the area around Kolwezi.

which could be trusted to undertake the most dangerous of missions.

On 17 May 1978, 2 REP was put on full alert for a possible operational deployment to Zaire. The most recent problems in this former Belgian colony, previously the Congo, had begun in 1976 with isolated incidents of civil unrest, but the area had a bloody history which went back even further. The Congo's independence in 1960 had been followed by the secession of Katanga — the country's richest province — from the state of Zaire. The following civil war resulted in the deaths of thousands of Africans and the murder of hundreds of European hostages.

In Kolwezi, shops were looted, women raped and passers-by murdered

In 1978 the country's population included a comparatively high proportion of white settlers who had remained after independence. Zaire is particularly rich in minerals and many whites had stayed on to run the mining industry. It was at one of these mining centres, Kolwezi — in the province of Shaba — where the civil unrest turned to rioting and then massacre. A column of some 1000 Katangan rebels broke across the border from their base in Angola, and seized the town. Joined by around 2000 guerrillas of the Congolese National Liberation Front (FNLC — *Front National pour la Libération du Congo*), the Katangan irregulars began to commit atrocities against the local population. In Kolwezi, shops were looted, commercial premises burned, women raped and anybody encountered on this bloody rampage, murdered out of hand. The rebels met with no resistance and began to turn their attention to their former colonisers. The future for more than 3000 European settlers and mining engineers, mostly French and Belgians, looked bleak indeed.

Zaire's armed forces were ill-equipped and powerless to intervene and Belgium, which had maintained an interest in the mining industry, was able to assist only in a 'humanitarian' role. Zaire's President Mobutu appealed to France for military assistance. It seemed as though the French and Belgian armed forces would mount a combined rescue operation but then came the news from French Intelligence that rebel radio traffic had been inter-

The far-off gaze of a battle-weary legionnaire at Kolwezi. By the time the Legion arrived on the scene, the Legion paras of 2 REP had gone two nights without sleep.

cepted, and that the Katangans were preparing to kill the European hostages before retreating across the border. France decided not to wait for the Belgian para-commandos — it was time for action.

In the early hours of 17 May, Lieutenant-colonel Erulin received a signal at 2 REP's headquarters at Calvi that his regiment was on six hours' notice of movement. Erulin was a remarkable man. A veteran of the Algerian war, he had achieved notoriety in the press for the methods he employed during the Battle of Algiers (1956-57). He became 2 REP's commander in July 1976 after having been in charge of the regiment's training section. He had worked hard to make 2 REP an efficient fighting force and during the operation his endeavours would reap rewards. At Kolwezi, 90% of the legionnaires had no previous experience of combat. However, Erulin was later to state, 'as soon as the first shot was fired, they all acted like veterans', vindicating the Legion's train hard, fight easy policy. Erulin himself died of a heart attack in September 1979 having left the regiment to take a posting with the general staff of the Air Force.

Silhouetted against the clear blue sky, they made perfect targets

The rescue mission was code-named Operation Leopard and within 25 hours of the initial alert the first Legion paratroops landed in the Zairean capital of Kinshasha. The first group of 650 Legion paras arrived in requisitioned civilian DC-8 airliners, after a flight of 6000km. On landing, they remained on the airfield, were issued their parachutes, re-packed their containers and other equipment, and emplaned. The Legion's tactical transport aircraft comprised one French *Armée de l'Air* C-160 Transall and four C-130 Hercules' belonging to Zaire's Air Force.

By midday on 19 May, 2 REP's first group took off from Kinshasha for the four-hour flight to Kolwezi. The first lift consisted of half the regiment's tactical HQ, and *1e, 2e* and *3e compagnies de combat* — a force numbering some 405 paratroopers, crammed into five aircraft. The second lift comprised the remainder of the TAC HQ, the recce section, the mortar section, and the 4e compagnie. This group remained on the tarmac at Kinshasha for the aircraft to return from dropping the first lift.

Surprise was essential and the entire operation was carried out in great secrecy. Any failure in maintaining security would undoubtedly have resulted in the Katangans massacring their hostages, so in Europe 'preparations' to send a rescue force were still underway. Then in mid-afternoon on 19 May 1978 the bluff ended. While media attention focused on the Belgian Para-Commandos preparing their equipment at Brussels airport, the first 450 legionnaires landed by parachute just outside Kolwezi. Their arrival was totally unexpected.

The selected DZ was the former Kolwezi Aero Club to the north-east of the Old Town. It was broad daylight as the first wave of legionnaires descended from the air. Silhouetted against the clear blue sky, they made perfect targets. Fortunately the Katangans were caught off guard and, despite the presence of small groups of rebels in the area, the landing was unopposed. After regrouping, the force divided up and set off through the elephant grass and termite hills towards their objectives. *3e compagnie* secured the main bridge leading from the New Town across to the east. *2e compagnie* meanwhile moved up towards the hospital and nearby mining complex which

The bodies of civilian casualties strewn along the road on the outskirts of Kolwezi testify to the suddeness and savagery of the terrorists' attack.

were situated about 2500m to the west of the DZ, while at the same time the 1e compagnie set off in a southerly direction towards the Jean XXIII school. Both the school and the hospital were vital objectives, and the pre-mission briefing had stressed that it was highly probable that these two buildings contained European hostages, guarded by Katangan rebels.

They came across evidence of the butchery that had already taken place

On their way to the school, hospital and mining complex the *1e* and *2e compagnies* began to come across evidence of the butchery that had already taken place. Civilian corpses, many of them women and children, lay stretched out on the streets and in surrounding houses. Many of the bodies had been savagely mutilated. In the face of such slaughter the legionnaires moved on, increasing the speed of their advance. In doing so they often ignored many of their SOPs, measures designed to protect them from possible ambush, in an effort to reach the hostages as quickly as possible. There was a real fear that any

delay could result in more civilians becoming victims of rebel atrocities.

As the legionnaires began to enter the more built-up areas they began to encounter resistance. After numerous fire-fights with FNLC groups they reached their primary objectives at dusk and were in position by dark. For some legionnaires, it was their third night without sleep, but there was still plenty of work to be done. The hostages were evacuated from the hospital during the night, and sporadic shooting continued throughout the hours of darkness. Most contacts with rebel groups were short-lived, lasting only a few minutes. The enemy were well-equipped but not well-trained, and when it came to fighting in a built-up area at night the Legion paras definitely had the advantage.

The *3e compagnie* had made its way to the east, rescued 30 Europeans about to be executed, and then gone on to secure the railway station, but not before they had been engaged by three Katangan machine-gun groups. Two of these were knocked out with a light anti-tank weapon, while the crew of the third withdrew to safety, taking their weapon with them. On occupying the station *3e compagnie* found a loaded ammunition train already

Legionnaires scan the surrounding countryside from the back of a captured vehicle. The Legion's own transport did not arrive until days after the operation began.

in residence, and had to arrange for its removal before moving on to the bridge.

Later that evening a larger rebel force, supported by two armoured cars and a truck, approached from the direction of the New Town, only to be engaged by legionnaires belonging to the *3e compagnie*, armed with a light anti-tank weapon and grenade launchers. The armoured vehicles were destroyed and the enemy's attempt to cross over failed.

The second wave of 2 REP paratroops jumped in at first light

At dawn on 20 May, the situation was still confused. The second wave of 2 REP paratroops jumped in at first light, with the *4e compagnie* landing on a DZ to the east of Kolwezi, while the remainder used the original DZ at the Aero Club. The second half of the TAC HQ, the recce section and the mortars, arrived safely, but the *4e compag-*

A weary Legion gunner rests against the butt of his machine gun while keeping a watchful eye open for any hostile activity in the surrounding bush.

nie came under intense enemy fire as soon as they landed. By this time *1e* and *2e compagnies de combat* had succeeded in clearing the southern and western quarters of the Old Town and the *2e compagnie* were able to offer its assistance in extricating the *4e compagnie*, which was by now pinned down.

Elsewhere, the fighting continued, especially in the suburbs. It was particularly fierce in northern area of Metalshaba, where the reconnaissance and mortar sections saw action shortly after landing. A force of some 300 Katangans had taken up positions in a metal factory some nine kilometres from the centre of town. The rebels felt confident enough to attack the Legion's leading section. In one action a column of Katangan infantry riding on lor-

ries, supported by two light tanks, mounted a counter-attack. The legionnaires, using mortars and anti-tank rocket launchers, set fire to the trucks and blew the tanks apart. The Katangans fled leaving 80 dead. Fighting in the area around the railway station and the road bridge to the New Town had been limited and, so Lieutenant-colonel Erulin brought the *3e compagnie* down south to clear the Manika estate. At the same time he established his TAC HQ in the Impala Hotel, the scene of a brutal massacre. Patrols were sent to search for survivors, and to collect released hostages for transportation to the nearby airfield.

It had been a gamble, but Operation Leopard was an unqualified success

Not all the hostages had been fortunate enough to be rescued by the legionnaires. In one building the Legion paras recovered the bodies of 38 men, women and children, mercilessly butchered by the FNLC rebels. To those taking part in the operation there was the constant fear of arriving in a place too late to stop such a massacre, and the thought that perhaps they could have saved more lives undoubtedly preyed on the minds of many legionnaires. It is unlikely that they could have and certainly if 2 REP had not managed to get there as fast as they did, or indeed if they had not been dispatched at all, the number of victims would have been very much higher.

By the afternoon of 20 May, the Belgian Para-Commandos had arrived and secured the nearby airfield, and Belgian medical teams were providing those rescued with food and medical aid prior to their evacuation. The following day the regiment's transport appeared. Nearly 100 of 2 REP's light vehicles, together with supplies and other support equipment, had been flown to Lubumbashi by US Air Force C-5 and C-141 transport aircraft. Lubumbashi was the closest air-head on to which the American aircraft could deliver 2 REP's second echelon. The vehicles completed the 240km journey on 21 May.

Their arrival at this time was fortuitous. By now the town had been cleared of rebels and the men were in desperate need of rest. After a short break, vehicle patrols were mounted and over the next seven days mobile groups scoured the surrounding area within a radius of 340km of Kolwezi, hunting down escaping rebels and searching for hostages on the outlying farms. The legionnaires were at risk from ambush all the time, and in one incident a party' returning from Kapata was fired on by two Katangans who leapt out in front of the vehicle and shattered its windscreen with automatic fire. The driver was equal to the situation, accelerating and running the men down. There was further fighting in Luilu and Kapata but the situation had been contained and the Legion was now firmly in control. By 28 May they had been pulled back to Lubumbashi and on 4 June 2 REP was back home at Camp Raffalli in Calvi. An African Multi-National Force arrived in Shaba on 8 June to ensure the safety of the civilian population.

Few other units would have been capable of conducting the operation

Operation Leopard was an unqualified success. It had justified the training and the role of 2 REP, and had proved the value of maintaining a quick reaction force capable of mounting an airborne assault. Few units, either in France or abroad, would have been capable of conducting such an operation. Even the Belgian Para-Commandos, in a far better position to mount such a mission than their British counter-parts, had taken 24 hours longer to arrive.

The French operation had undoubtedly been something of a gamble, but it was one that had paid dividends. It was the first operational airborne deployment by French troops since 1956, when together with the British paras, they had landed at Suez. Between 1946 and 1958 France had been involved in nearly 160 airborne operations involving almost 60,000 men, and was clearly the most experience country in this area of warfare. However, 20 years had passed and this particular mission was unlike any other they had previously undertaken.

The speed with which the operation had been mounted restricted all but the most elementary planning and presented 2 REP with a number of severe problems. Timing was crucial if lives were to be saved. The regiment was put on six hours notice to move on the morning of 17 May. At 2000 hours that evening 2 REP, much of which had been away training, assembled and was ready

Armed with a captured AK-47 asault rifle, a mortar-group commander supervises his group's fire support mission during Operation Leopard.

Legionnaires hold suspected terrorists at gunpoint during mopping up operations at Kolwezi. The main battle lasted two days, but securing the area was a lengthier task.

to move. By 0130 hours on 18 May, the regiment was ready to move and by 0800 hours that morning it was in position to be airlifted out of Solenzara airport, Corsica. It is highly doubtful they could have been any quicker.

There were too few aircraft to complete the drop in one wave

Just as impressive as the speed of the response was the manner in which potentially disastrous problems were overcome. For example, the main force arrived at Kinshasha airfield shortly after 2300 hours on 18 May to find that the only parachutes available were US T-10s, a type of parachute with which the legionnaires were unfamiliar, and which did not have the attachments to which they could affix their personal equipment containers. Then it was discovered that there were too few aircraft to complete the regiment's drop in one wave and that the force would have to divide into two separate groups. Part of the TAC HQ and all of the regiment's support weapons would have to remain behind until the second lift. In addition the vehicles and heavy stores would have to be air-landed some 240km away from the target, severely restricting the regiment's mobility for at least two days and possibly longer.

Intelligence available as to the size and location of the rebel forces, and the general situation in Kolwezi, was also limited. Their estimated strength, given to the legionnaires in a briefing by an officer from the French Military Mission in Kinshasha, was anywhere from 1500 to more than 4000. 2 REP had little to go on. They would be required to jump from 600 feet, on to an unprepared and unmarked DZ, with no external support and without their own heavy weapons, and to then fight an unknown enemy while at the same time attempting to rescue hostages whose exact whereabouts were unknown.

The T-10 parachute harnesses had to be adapted with wire and para-cord so that the legionnaires' equipment containers could be released prior to landing. Failure to do this would result in broken legs or worse, and this gave the men yet one more thing to worry about. The Hercules transport aircraft were different from the

Opposite: The carnage of war. Civilian casualties (above) were heavy, although the arrival of the Legion prevented a massacre. Kolwezi town itself (below) suffered badly.

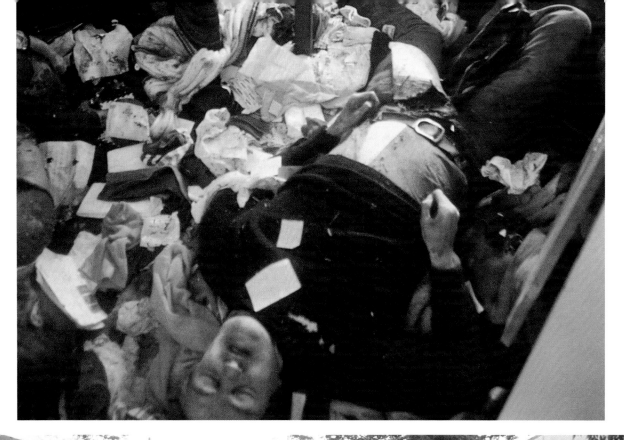

Transalls from which 2 REP usually jumped, and unfamiliarity leads to increased risks. The legionnaires were fortunate to have some experienced French instructors, attached to the Zairean Air Force, who were familiar with the equipment and were able to offer the Legion paras good advice.

The drop went well, despite the leading wave being dropped too high

The aircrews flying the mission were less experienced. A paratroop operation requires a great deal of skill; 'meatball' drops, unlike bombs, do not descend in a straight line once released and allowances have to be made for height, airspeed and cross-winds. In the event, the lead aircraft made a 'navigational' error and had to be brought back on course after being chased by the remaining Transall, which was acting as the mission's Command and Control ship. But the drop went well, despite the leading wave being dropped too high and one man becoming 'hung up' by his static-line. The Legion's thorough training paid dividends; the unfortunate legionnaire kept his head and managed to deploy his reserve 'chute after being cut away by a quick-thinking despatcher.

The area in and around Kolwezi was brought under control

Once on the ground, the operation went well. The rebels were rooted out, those hostages still alive were rescued, and the area in and around Kolwezi was brought under control. Despite the second drop, due to take place on the late afternoon/early evening of 20 May, being postponed until the following morning, the first element of 2 REP achieved its primary aims within hours of landing. They did this with no external support whatsoever. When the Belgians arrived at Kolwezi the situation was already in hand and the Para-Commandos and Belgian medical teams could begin their task of evacuating the European population, many of whom would not have been alive had it not been for the decisive action taken by France and the Legion.

The Belgians' role was 'humanitarian' and it has been suggested that little love was lost between them and the French. Certainly the communication between the two forces was minimal and Colonel Gras, the French Army officer in overall command of the operation, was later reported as saying the Belgian commander did not advise

him of his forces' arrival, or indeed of their departure. The Para-commandos had air-landed some distance from the town at Kolwezi airport, an airfield which had previously been secured by a Zairean parachute battalion. The Belgian forces were not involved in the fighting, although their presence in the town did allow the legionnaires to get on with their job of hunting down the rebels in the surrounding countryside.

Operation Leopard succeeded largely because of the bold tactics and aggressive fighting skills employed by the men of 2 REP. They accounted for 247 rebels dead and a further 163 FNLC members captured. They recovered or destroyed two armoured vehicles, 21 rocket launchers, 15 mortars, 10 heavy/medium machine guns and more than 250 small arms. This was at a cost of five legionnaires killed and 25 wounded. The French Military Mission to Zaire was also involved in the operation and lost a total of six men killed or missing in action. The Zairean paratroopers, who had bravely seized Kolwezi airfield prior to the arrival of any of their allies, lost 14 dead and eight wounded. Civilian casualties were heavier and included 120 Europeans and over 500 Zairois. But these last figures are far smaller than they would have been had the French not agreed to President Mobutu's request for assistance.

It had proved itself to be a rapid reaction force in every sense of the word

The brilliant action at Kolwezi brought worldwide praise for the men of 2 REP. The regiment received its seventh citation in Army orders. It had triumphantly proved itself to be a rapid reaction force in every sense of the phrase, and its success had reinforced French military credibility. The prestige of 2 REP soared. Thanks to Kolwezi the regiment earned itself a reputation as one of the West's most potent and flexible intervention units, every inch the equal of the American airborne forces and the British Parachute Regiment. Competition to join 2 REP is extremely tough and the regiment ensures it gets only the very best recruits. It turns those men into fearsome, highly-trained fighting machines, on constant alert ready to go into action anywhere in the world.

Opposite: Locally-raised defence forces patrol after the battle for Kolwezi. Operation Leopard proved that with 2 REP, the Legion had a first-rate fighting outfit.

WHY THE FOREIGN LEGION?

The Legion may seem an anachronism in the modern world of national armies, but its history reveals just why it has been, and continues to be, so important to France. And, as the warfare of the past half-century has shown, many other countries have found that formations composed of foreigners can often do a superb job; Britain's Gurkhas, the Rhodesian Light Infantry and the South African Commandos have all experienced considerable success in hard fighting.

'The *Légion Etrangère* is an integrated element of the regular French army and it is not, nor has it ever been, a mercenary formation. Mercenaries fight for money, the Legion fights for France. Its troops are paid a salary equivalent to that received by many other professional military formations. They sign a five-year contract, and are not "freelance" soldiers undertaking one particular mission.' (Legion Commandant General).

The *Légion Etrangère* owes it origins to an order

Practice on the firing range. While the Legion still prides itself on toughness and durability, weapons and technical skills have become increasingly important in recent years.

that he could muster a force of foreign volunteers to fight for France in Algeria. This would solve the problem of what to do with the foreigners who infested his country, at the same time as releasing French troops to maintain order at home.

News travelled quickly and volunteers came forward in larger numbers

Louis Philippe found an ally in the form of a freelance Belgian adventurer named Lacroix, the self-styled Baron Boegard who, according to contemporary reports, was already in the process of forming companies comprising volunteers from all walks of life to fight alongside the French army and colonise Algeria. It was Lacroix's suggestion that France's poorer and unwanted foreign settlers could be conscripted into this new 'Legion', a view which met with the full agreement of the French King and was formalised by royal decree on 9 March 1831. Signed by the monarch and with the support of the French Minister for War, Maréchal Soult, the royal order stated that:

1.	Such a Legion should be employed only outside the borders of continental France.

2.	All applicants should be aged between 18 and 40, and not less than 5ft tall.

3.	All applicants should be furnished with a birth certificate, a testimonial of good conduct, and documentary evidence from a military authority stating that they possessed the necessary requirements to make a good soldier in the Legion.

In addition, the order also laid down that the uniform would be a blue long-tailed coat bordered with red facings, red trousers and a heavy black shako worn on the head — standard French army infantry dress for the period. The famous white *képi* would be introduced in 1841 for operations in North Africa.

A recruitment depot was established, with enlistment centres set up in the provinces manned by *sous-officiers* who, it appears, paid scant regard to the articles laid down in the Royal decree. Providing there was no obvious evidence of physical disability almost all applicants were accepted. News of the lack of rigid entry requirements travelled quickly and volunteers came forward in

signed by the French King Louis Philippe in 1831, which stated that a '*légion composée d'étrangers*' should be created for service abroad.' Louis Philippe's decision was a politically expedient method of dealing with the many political refugees and fugitives from justice who had sought sanctuary in his realm. In addition, there was a multitude of unemployed soldiers in Paris, including men of the disbanded royal bodyguard and the Regiment of Hohenlohe.

France was filled with exiles from wars and uprisings throughout Europe

The new formation was regarded by his High Command as being of dubious quality. However, Louis Philippe had good reason to doubt the security of his regency in the revolution-ridden first half of the 19th century. France was filled with exiles from uprisings and civil wars throughout Europe at a time when France itself was conducting a war in North Africa. Louis Philippe reasoned

great numbers. Within days a second order was issued which forbade the recruitment of French nationals, and or married men without special authorisation. The order was ineffective as Frenchmen simply became 'Belgians'. These volunteers, together with many former inmates of French prisons, 'volunteered' by their respective local authorities, were shipped to North Africa.

Discipline was established by Colonel Stoffel, a hard-bitten Swiss veteran

After a somewhat chaotic start in which drunkenness and desertion were rife, and attacks on officers were not uncommon, discipline was finally established by Colonel Stoffel, a hard-bitten Swiss veteran. Using experienced ex-regular troops, mostly from old Prussian and Swiss regiments, Stoffel enforced his authority and by 1832 had built up a force that had begun to resemble a military formation. At first his troops were considered fit only for pioneer duties and were put to work constructing blockhouses and building roads.

The new *Legién Etrangère* was initially organised into five battalions, each with its own individual national identity. The first battalion comprised Swiss Guard and Hohenlohe veterans; the second and third, Swiss and German volunteers; the fourth, Spaniards; and the fifth, Sicilians, Sardinians and Italians. In 1833 and 1834 the sixth and seventh battalions were raised, comprising Belgians and Dutch, and Poles respectively.

The Legion's first action was fought on 27 April 1832 near Algiers

The battalions themselves were organised along the same lines as those of the French line infantry battalions, with eight companies of 112 men each. The *Légion Etrangère* possessed its own *compagnies d'élite*, with each battalion having a company of grenadiers and a company of *voltigeurs,* as well as normal infantry. Grenadiers were usually the biggest and strongest men of the battalion and acted as shock troops, *voltigeurs* acted as scouts and skirmishers.

As the *Légion Etrangère* began to take shape in Algeria it started to acquire its own individual identity. Its first

King Louis Philippe, who founded the Foreign Legion on 10 March 1831. Within five years the Legion had torn itself apart in the Carlist wars in Spain.

action was fought on 27 April 1832 at a place called Maison Carrée, a few miles from Algiers. Men of the 3rd Battalion succeeded in driving a group of Arabs from a building, which was subsequently turned into a Legion outpost. In the next month a Legion detachment was to take part in an action which was to typify those which were to follow in other campaigns in other countries. A 28-man patrol commanded by a Swiss lieutenant named Cham was caught out in the open near Maison Carrée.

Their bodies were mutilated and their genitals were hacked off

Heavily out-numbered by Algerian rebels, they were attacked, overrun and wiped-out. Cham became the first Legion officer to die in battle. Their bodies were mutilated and their genitals were hacked-off. The fact that these men had lost their lives 'in the service of France' did not go unnoticed. The French Army's commander in North Africa, General Camille-Alphonse Trezel, publicly proclaimed their achievement with the words 'the soldiers of

the Foreign Regiment showed great bravery in battle, as they have shown a particular disposition to endure fatigue, heat and other privations, without appearing to suffer'. The Legion was now beginning to be taken more seriously and the battalions of foreigners, originally the object of derision, came to be seen as an exceptionally useful military tool.

As an article of policy, Legion casualty figures, with the notable exception of its officers, were not announced and often went unrecorded. This meant that even approximate casualties sustained by the Legion during its early years are unknown, but they were undoubtedly high. The Legion, then as today, was tasked with the more difficult and dangerous missions, such as defending isolated outposts or leading advancing columns through enemy-held territory. However, while the military soon began to appreciate the value of its foreign regiments, the

General Rollet, first Inspector of the Foreign Legion and known as 'Father of the Legion' for his work in helping to create the modern Legion.

French government in Paris was more difficult to convince. In July 1835 the Legion was ceded to Spain in its entirety, and in August 123 officers and 4021 legionnaires landed in Tarragona to support France's ally Queen Isabella against the revolutionary forces led by her uncle, Don Carlos. The following three years proved disastrous for the Legion as it withered away through combat, desertion, disease, maladministration, lack of logistical support and a lack of proper leadership.

Many of those who survived Spain signed on with the second Legion

By the end of 1838, the Legion that had fought in the Carlist War was disbanded, with only 500 surviving. The total casualty figures sustained by the Legion are in fact even worse than they first appear. Throughout the war additional volunteers had been recruited and dispatched to Spain, so many more legionnaires died than were sent at the beginning. Of the officers, 23 died and 109 were wounded, and of the legionnaires some 3600 were killed or died later of their wounds or from disease. The number of legionnaires that were wounded is not recorded but it is estimated that about 4000 deserted. Many of those who did survive signed on with the second Legion that had been raised by a royal decree dated 16 December 1835. The new Legion was sent to Algeria in early 1837. A serious gap in France's army in North Africa had been created by the removal of the 4000-strong first Legion in 1835. The French government were not to make the same mistake twice and, although it has since undergone incalculable changes in structure and organisation, the Legion's essential character and — above all — its spirit, has remained the same.

Napoleon's army of 1812 contained more foreigners than Frenchmen

The use of foreign troops was not in any way unusual. Long before the creation of the *Légion Etrangère* France had employed foreign soldiers in her armies. The Valois kings were protected by Scots Guards, the Bourbons had their regiments of German, English and Irish professional soldiers. The Swiss, used extensively by the French and others, suffered heavily at the hands of the Paris mobs while defending Louis XVI during the French Revolution.

During the First Empire Napoleon realised his territorial ambitions required more manpower than France could provide, and by the time he invaded Russia in 1812 his army contained more foreigners than Frenchmen. During his later 'Hundred Days' campaign in 1815, Napoleon raised eight foreign regiments under the title 'Royal Foreign Legion'. However, none of these were ready when he encountered the British at Waterloo, and at the battle he had only one Swiss formation under his command.

France made extensive use of the armies of countries conquered

The increase in compulsory enlistment lessened the need for mercenaries. During the French Revolutionary and Napoleonic wars the number of mercenary troops decreased drastically, as the *levée en masse* was introduced, and France made extensive use of the armies of the countries she had conquered. However by the time the French Army met the British at Waterloo, Napoleon faced more 'foreign' troops than British, since Wellington's Army of 67,000 included some 43,000 foreigners the King's German Legion, Hanoverians, Nassauers and Dutch-Belgians.

In the post-Napoleonic era there were further increases in conscript armies, as the power of the nation state increased and populations became generally more patriotic. This was accompanied with a corresponding reduction in the employment of foreign troops, who were viewed as being unreliable, generally lacking in patriotic motives and certainly more expensive.

Spain also recruited outside help to fight its battles

The major powers retained the use of colonial troops, their primary purpose being to police and defend any occupied territories. Colonial duties were the main reason behind Britain's use of the Gurkhas for instance, and without Algeria it is doubtful whether France would have required its Foreign Legion. Spain — once a major world power but by the 19th-century divided and destabilised by successive internal and external struggles — recruited outside help to fight her battles. Between 1834 and 1839 the first 'Spanish Legion', raised under special authority

A legionnaire serving in Dahomey, West Africa, around 1892. As the Great Powers scrambled for Africa, the Legion was an essential tool in France's policy of colonial expansion.

by Britain's government, was dispatched to Spain to fight in the Carlist Wars. It was not until the 20th century, however, that a permanent Legion of foreigners was established in Spain.

General Franco was one of the Legion's first officers

The Spanish Foreign Legion was modelled on its older French conterpart and therefore shares a number of similarities with it. Formed in 1920 by Colonel José Millan Astray, the Spanish Foreign Legion's raison d'etre was Spanish Morocco. Major Franco, later to become Generalissimo and leader of his country, was one of its first officers and between 1920-23 served as its deputy commander, and as its commanding officer between 1923-27. The Legion fought extensively in North Africa and its success led to Franco's promotion to Brigadier-General. During the Spanish Civil War (1936-39) the Legion was expanded to 18 battalions and proved an invaluable weapon to Franco. However, the Spanish

The Spanish Foreign Legion was established in emulation of France's Legion and organised along the same lines. Nowadays, however, all recruits must be Spanish nationals.

Legion suffered heavily during the bitter and bloody struggle, losing nearly half its officers and over a third of its legionnaires, almost 8000 casualties (killed or died of wounds) in all. After the fascist victory, Franco returned the Legion to Morocco where it remained until that country gained its independence in 1956. The Legion stayed in Africa until Spain's withdrawal from the Sahara in 1976, when it returned home for the first time since the end of the Civil War.

Millan Astray, the first commander of La Legion, possessed great physical courage and an almost unbelievable indifference to death. He was, above all, 'a soldier's soldier'; in the course of his military career he was wounded on five separate occasions and lost both his left leg and one eye. He was decorated dozens of times, and his awards included France's *Légion d'Honneur*. Millan Astray adopted many French Foreign Legion ideas, including that of forming a close, family-like bond between legionnaires and their officers. Discipline in the early Spanish Legion was, if anything, even harsher than in France's. Millan Astray also stressed the importance of

maintaining traditional links with past achievements. His battle cry of '*Viva la muerte!*' — Long live death! — has a definite Legion ring to it, and his artificial left leg and eye, which now reside at La Legion's museum at Ceuta, are treated with the same kind of reverence accorded to Capitaine Danjou's hand at Aubagne.

Spain's Legion is the most capable formation in Spain's armed forces

Like France's *Légion Etrangère*, Spain's Legion has taken on a new role in recent years. It represents the toughest, most capable formation within Spain's armed forces and is currently in the process of being reorganised into the *Fuerza de Intervencion Rapida*, a rapid deployment force equivalent to France's *Force d'Action Rapide*. The Legion consists of 7000 men divided into three *Tercios,* or regiments. The first and second *Tercios* garrison Spain's remaining outposts in North Africa, Ceuta and Melilla, which are on the coast of Morocco. The third *Tercio* is based in the Canary Islands and comprises two motorised battalions *(banderas)* and one light infantry battalion. Both North African regiments comprise one mechanised and one motorised infantry battalion.

The Legion's elite Special Operations Unit, based at

Ronda in the Sierra Nevada mountain range, consists of two airborne infantry banderas, which include the *Bandera de Operaciones Especiales* (BOEL), Spain's Special Operations Battalion, a unit with a similar role and training to France's 2 REP. All Spanish Foreign Legion units are well trained, and they maintain a high standard of discipline.

Recruits have ranged from common criminals to White Russian princes

Unlike their French counterparts, the Spanish Legion was traditionally composed mainly of Spaniards, who enlisted for a minimum period, in La Legion's case three years, with an option on five. Recently, the minimum enlistment period had been reduced to 18 months which, although it is six months longer than that required by the remainder of the Spanish Army, is substantially less than that demanded by the French. In addition, the recruitment of foreigners has now ceased; whereas in the past a volunteer would be able to qualify for entry on presentation of any passport, volunteers must now be able to prove their Spanish origins.

During its 70-year history Spain's Legion has recruited a diverse selection of recruits ranging from common criminals to White Russian princes, from former SS members to ex-OAS men from Algeria. Despite its origins as a mercenary force the Spanish Foreign Legion is highly respected by traditionalists, and maintains close links with Spanish Catholic institutions. Each year a Legion company crosses from Ceuta in North Africa to march in the religious processions at Malaga. They carry with them a crucifix of the Legion's religious patron — El Cristo de la Buena Muerte — the Christ of the Good Death. In the last five years the Spanish Army, and the Legion in particular has been reorganised and modernised. But while its training and tactics may change, its traditions remain strongly entrenched.

Another traditional military formation composed of foreigners in the service of another state are Britain's Gurkhas. The ties which bind the Gurkha hill-tribesmen from Nepal to the British Army are long-standing and close. In 1813 and 1816 Britain's forces in India fought two short but fierce wars against the Kingdom of Nepal.

Spain's Legion has been transformed into a modern rapid intervention force, highly trained, well-equipped and organised to go into action at a moment's notice.

The eventual British victory was hard won and the fighting resulted in strong mutual respect for each side's abilities. This respect resulted in three Gurkha infantry battalions being raised, and Gurkha soldiers have served the British Crown loyally ever since.

During the Indian Mutiny the Gurkha regiments remained faithful

During the Indian Mutiny (1857-8), when native troops of Britain's Indian Army rebelled against the Crown, the Gurkha regiments remained faithful. They fought for the British during both World Wars and, by the end of World War Two, numbered almost 250,000. When the British departed the Indian sub-continent in 1947, the Gurkhas regiments were divided between the new, independent Indian Army and the British Army. Following their move to the British Army five Gurkha infantry battalions, 2nd, 6th, 7th (two battalions) and 10th Gurkha Rifles, were augmented by additional support units including engineers, signals and transport.

The Gurkha battalions played a major role in Britain's 'small wars', notably the counter-insurgency campaigns in Malaya and Borneo, where their reputation as tough jungle fighters was significantly enhanced. The most recent conflict in which Gurkhas were involved was Britain's campaign in the South Atlantic. During the Falklands War between Britain and the Argentine in 1982, The 1st Battalion 7th Duke of Edinburgh's Own Gurkha Rifles (1/7 GR) were held in reserve for the final assault on Port Stanley, the major Argentinian stronghold and Britain's main objective.

Like the Legion, Gurkhas take the 'military family' concept very seriously

The mere presence of Gurkha troops had a deeply disturbing psychological effect on the Argentine defenders, among whom rumours of their ruthlessness and superb close-fighting ability abounded. The fact that the campaign ended before the Gurkha battalion was committed

Below: This Spanish Legion exercise uses live ammunition, guaranteeing that the that training will be as close as possible to the real thing. Opposite: Recruits to Britain's Brigade of Gurkhas line up for inspection.

Although they are drawn from Nepal, in the foothills of the Himalayas, the Gurkhas have acquired a well-deserved reputation as superb jungle troops.

to the assault had not lessened their reputation, although it did cause considerable disappointment among the troops themselves.

Like the Legion, Gurkhas take the 'military family' concept very seriously, with many sons following in the footsteps of their fathers, grandfathers and great-grandfathers. Competition to join the Gurkha battalions (both British and Indian) is fierce, with a case of too many young men chasing too few available positions. Initial recruiting is conducted by *gallah-wallahs*, former Gurkha NCOs who travel Nepal looking for likely candidates. They work on a commission basis, receiving a bounty for every man they select who is eventually signed up. The young tribesmen are able to volunteer from the age of 17, and enlist for a minimum of 15 years.

The principal Gurkha formation is currently based at Sek Kong Camp in Hong Kong's New Territories. The Gurkha Field Force (the equivalent to a Brigade) consists of four Gurkha infantry battalions plus service support. A fifth battalion is stationed near Aldershot in England, and is one of the two British infantry battalions in 5 Airmobile Brigade, tasked with the air-landing role.

The Sultan of Brunei pays for the resident Gurkha battalion himself

A small nucleus of Gurkhas are now parachute-trained, maintaining a tradition of Gurkha airborne soldiers which began during World War Two and ended with the reduction of Britain's Gurkha forces following the British withdrawal from India.

Another rotational posting for the Gurkha battalions is Brunei. The Sultan of Brunei, one of the richest men in the world, pays for the resident Gurkha battalion himself,

Heavily-camouflaged and deep in concentration, a Gurkha soldier takes aim through the SUSAT sights on his SA80 personal weapon.

Anti-guerrilla warfare can call for an unconventional approach; South African Recce Commandos in Namibia found that horses could be an efficient means of transport.

not only lessening the burden on Britain's defence budget, and also giving the Gurkhas an ideal opportunity to fine-tune their jungle warfare skills. Their renowned ability to operate within a jungle environment comes through training, commitment and adaptability rather than from childhood experience. Nepal is a mountain kingdom, far removed from the thick, inhospitable jungles of Burma, Malaya or Borneo, countries where the Gurkhas earned their reputation. Skills are passed on from one generation of soldiers to the next, beginning at the start of the Gurkha's basic nine-month training course and continuing for the rest of his military career.

Should the Gurkhas be 'sold off' it would be a sad loss for Britain

The future of Britain's Gurkhas is once again uncertain. They are the last remnant of the units raised by the British to police their Empire; as the colonies gained their independence so the need for colonial regiments diminished. The debate to retain the five battalions began during India's post-war struggle for independence and has continued through each successive defence cut that has followed. Britain is due to leave Hong Kong in 1997 and this could result in the Gurkhas losing their primary reason

for existing as part of the British Army. Should the Gurkha battalions be 'sold off' to the Sultanate of Brunei, or to the Indian government, it would be a sad loss for Britain, the country they have served loyally for nearly two centuries, but an undoubted gain for their new employers.

France's Foreign Legion regiments remain among the very few units of any world army that employ foreign nationals. The British Army for instance, accept only Nepalese recruits into the Gurkha Rifle battalions, and Spain's Legion has now closed its doors to non-Spanish nationals. The only competition that the Legion has had in the last 20 years has been from the Rhodesian Light Infantry.

The RLI was at the forefront of Rhodesia's war against guerrillas

During the two World Wars most major powers recruited foreigners to fight on their behalf. Colonial troops were extensively employed by France and Britain during World

War One, and from the early days of World War Two Britain was well supported by her Commonwealth. Australian, Canadian and New Zealand forces joined with the Indian Army and units raised from Britain's colonial territories in a combined effort to defeat the armies of the Axis powers. One of the countries to provide Britain with military support during World War Two was Rhodesia (now Zimbabwe) in southern Africa.

Commandos operated as a 'Fire Force', on immediate standby

Rhodesia continued to maintain close ties with Britain after the war and a Rhodesian SAS Squadron was raised to fight alongside their British counterparts during the Malayan Emergency. Its first commander was a 24 year old acting major named Peter Walls, who later became the commanding officer of the 1st Battalion The Rhodesian Light Infantry. The RLI was at the forefront of Rhodesia's war against guerrillas throughout the 'bush-

war' that began with Rhodesia's unilateral declaration of independence (UDI) in 1965 until after the Lancaster House agreement in 1979. Lieutenant Colonel (later Lieutenant General) Walls reorganised the RLI on a commando system.

During the latter stages of the war the RLI became increasingly involved in 'external' operations, carrying the battle across Rhodesia's borders and conducting lightening strikes on 'terr' training camps in the neighbouring states of Zambia and Mozambique. When not involved in 'externals' the Commandos operated as a 'Fire Force', on immediate standby to deploy wherever needed. Fire Force 'sticks' would be inserted after an 'incident', such as a vehicle ambush, land-mine explosion or contact, and carry out the follow-up operation. 'Sticks' of four to eight men would either be parachuted in from a low-flying DC-

Many of South Africa's soldiers came battle-hardened from service with units such as the Rhodesian Light Infantry — itself a force containing a large number of foreigners.

3 Dakota or 'Dak', or air-lifted by Alouette helicopters. The troopers of the RLI Commandos were all parachute trained but there was something else special about them — a high percentage were 'foreign'.

RLI troopers represented over 50 different nationalities

For the RLI was, in effect, Rhodesia's foreign legion. At one time RLI troopers represented over 50 different nationalities including, it was reported, an Eskimo. There were, however, two major differences between this unit and the French Foreign Legion. Firstly, the RLI conducted most of its operations within and around Rhodesia's borders and was raised to defend the homeland. In addition, it was not raised specifically to attract foreign nationals to its ranks, that it did so was because the RLI was an attractive proposition for professional soldiers and Rhodesia was in desperate need of men to fight the war. Active overseas recruiting was, of course, out of the question, and most volunteers heard of the RLI by word of mouth. The money, though not much, went a long way, and the

chance for action was constant and continuous. Time off was also good and a trooper could expect to spend an average of a month in the field followed by about 20 days R&R. In the ranks of the RLI you could find 'Brits' who had served in Northern Ireland, Americans and Australians who had done tours in Vietnam, Canadians, Germans, Dutchmen, Frenchmen and even former French Foreign legionnaires. Providing a man was fit, healthy and could speak English there was nothing to stop him from volunteering.

Like the Foreign Legion, the RLI conducted its own basic training, regardless of an individual's previous military experience. After signing on the dotted line a man would be re-imbursed his air-fare and sent to Llewellin Barracks, Bulawayo, for training. The initial course conducted by Depot Rhodesia Regiment (DRR) lasted for eight weeks. At the end of this period men would be selected for officer training, either with the RLI or the Rhodesian SAS. The remainder, including the majority of national servicemen, would stay at DRR while those chosen for the RLI or the SAS would join their units for further training.

The RLI offered an escape from the boredom of peacetime soldiering

Life in the RLI was, without doubt, exciting. The war in Rhodesia was fought at a time of 'world peace', when NATO armies trained for an increasingly unlikely war in western Europe. Vietnam had fallen to the communists and the United States of America was reducing the size of their armed forces. The world had little to offer the professional soldier searching for a place to practise his skills — even life in the Foreign Legion was relatively quiet. An initial two year contract with the Rhodesian Security Forces offered an escape from the boredom of peacetime soldiering, in much the same way as the Legion does today.

The only option left seems to be the boat-train to Calais

The Rhodesian Light Infantry Commandos were disbanded in 1980 after the transition to majority rule. There could be no place in the new Zimbabwe for a unit of white mercenaries which had fought so hard to preserve the old order.

The Spanish Foreign Legion now solely accepts volunteers from among its citizenry and the only way to become a Gurkha is to have been born in the Himalayan foothills of Nepal, and then to win one of the few places available in the British Army. Nowadays, the only option left for those seeking a life of military adventure abroad seems to be the boat-train to Calais and a visit to the French Foreign Legion's recruiting centres.

Travelling light to aid rapid movement, but still heavily-armed, these South African commandos warily approach a suspected guerrilla position in the bush.

THE FUTURE OF THE LEGION

Does the *Légion Etrangère* have a secure future within France's armed forces? And will the modern world continue to provide a stream of men willing to sign away five years of their lives in return for the coveted white *képi* and a life of adventure?

Over the past decade the armed forces of many western nations have reorganised their airborne and amphibious units into highly mobile, quick-reaction forces capable of conducting out-of-area (OOA) operations. As it looks to the future, the French Foreign Legion increasingly sees itself as fitting into this role, to provide France with the kind of swift strike force that many other countries now believe is essential. The United States of America's Rapid Deployment Force (RDF), spearheaded by the 82nd Airborne Division — which possesses a total strength of around 18,000 troops — is 'on call' to be deployed to

Combat swimmers of 2 REP prepare to make a low-level jump, without parachutes, from a helicopter. 2 REP in particular has broadened the range of the Legion's specialisations.

trouble spots anywhere in the world. The US military clearly demonstrated its ability to mount out-of-area operations during Operation Urgent Fury, the American invasion of the Caribbean island of Grenada in October 1983. Operation Desert Shield, mounted in August 1990 to defend Saudi Arabia against possible Iraqi aggression, involved even greater numbers of troops with attendant logistical complications, but was carried out smoothly and with a minimum of problems.

In 1982, Britain's Falklands campaign in the South Atlantic had highlighted the need for an adequately equipped, suitably structured force capable of conducting a long-range combined-arms operation. As a result of this experience, the British Army created 5 Airborne Brigade in October 1983. The benefits of possessing this type of

Opposite page: A member of 2 REP's anti-terrorist unit, FA-MAS and walkie-talkie slung across his chest. Below: These legionnaires, guns at the ready, have just disembarked from a French Air Force Puma helicopter. The Legion pioneered the use of helicopters, in Algeria in the 1950s.

specialised fighting force were a lesson that did not go unheeded by other western nations.

Following the Falklands war in 1982 and Grenada in 1983, the next major out-of-area operation launched by the West began at the end of 1989, when the United States government committed elements of its Rapid Deployment Force to Panama in order to depose General Manuel Noriega.

Widespread looting broke out in Gabon. The Legion was put on alert

On 20 December 1989, approximately 11,500 American troops assaulted 27 different targets. The operation was code-named 'Just Cause' and was the largest night-time operation undertaken since World War Two. Some units involved were already in place as part of an agreement to secure the Panama Canal Zone, but others, such as 82nd Airborne Division, had to travel 1400 miles to the operational area. Despite the Americans' difficulties in locating and capturing Noriega himself, the operation was widely

estimated to have been both a military and a logistical success.

More recently, civil unrest in Gabon prompted the French government to deploy troops to protect the lives of French residents in that country. Gabon is a former French territory on the west coast of Africa, bordered to the north by Cameroon and to the east and south by the Congo. On 22 May 1990, the body of an opposition leader was discovered in a Libreville hotel. This prompted riots against President Omar Bongo's administration and the situation, unstable since March 1990, became rapidly worse. General civil unrest followed the murder, representing the most serious threat to date to Bongo's 23 years of autocratic rule, and widespread looting broke out throughout Gabon. French interests were felt to be threatened and the Legion was put on standby. The following day, 23 May, Operation Requin (Shark) began.

Once alerted, 2 REP and 2 REI selected personnel to join a task force under the command of General Janvier,

Left: A member of 2 REP glides down to earth, his rucksack slung beneath him. Below: An AMX-10RC reconnaissance vehicle of 1 REC, equipped with its 105mm cannon, seen during Exercise Kecker-Spatz in September 1987.

himself a former commanding officer of 2 REP. Two companies from 2 REI together with the *Etat Major Tactique* (EMT) or Tactical HQ, moved to Nîmes airport, a short drive from their base in southern France.

It clearly demonstrated the Legion's ability to deploy troops rapidly

This force was joined by a company of Legion paratroops from 2 REP, and the combined formation was flown out of Nîmes on 24 May 1990. The speed with which this rescue mission was mounted provides a good example of the Legion's state of readiness, especially when one considers that 24 May was a public holiday in France!

While the Legion units were on their way to Libreville another force, comprising elements of 8 RPIMa, the regular marine paratroops, left N'Djamena, Chad, where they were conducting a routine training exercise, and made for Port Gentil on the Gabonese coast. By 25 May both the Legion companies and those from 8 RPIMa were in position. The safety of French residents assured, France's Minister of Co-operation, M. Jacques Pelletier stated, from Paris, 'the government has taken the necessary steps to allow French citizens to leave Port Gentil if they so desire.' On 25 May France air-lifted 800 of its 3000 citizens from the Port Gentil and the oil-terminal was secured.

Operation Requin was a major success. It clearly demonstrated France's, and more particularly the Legion's, ability to deploy troops rapidly over a considerable distance. The breakdown of civil order in Gabon was forestalled and within two months the French task force was withdrawn.

Foreign Legion paras and other French airborne units have also operated under the flag of the United Nations. Beirut was the setting for a major UN peacekeeping operation, beginning in the late 1970s. The first French troops

The Legion's detachment to the UN forces prepares to disembark in France after a tour in Beirut, where their job was to supervise the evacuation of PLO forces from the city.

to enter this high-profile military/political arena were RPIMa paratroops, who joined the international peacekeeping force in the Levant in 1978. The first Legion paras from 2 REP arrived in Lebanon in August 1982, the end result of a resolution presented by the French government to the UN Security Council. In simple terms, the French presented a case that all foreign troops in the Lebanon should be withdrawn, and that this evacuation should be reinforced by troops of the International Peacekeeping Force.

2 REP provided security for PLO personnel leaving Beirut

After lengthy negotiations Yasser Arafat, leader of the Palestine Liberation Organisation (PLO), agreed to the proposal on condition that French troops supervised the operation and that they be permitted to retain their personal weapons. The paras of 2 REP were chosen for this mission and on the evening of 18/19 August a detachment departed Calvi for the British base at Larnaca,

Cyprus. The 2 REP 'peacekeepers' were tasked with providing physical security for PLO personnel departing Beirut under the direction of the Lebanese army, assuring the security of the local population during the operation and supporting the restoration of Lebanese governmental authority in the area.

Operation Epaulard 1 (Killer Whale) was underway, and from Larnaca the 2 REP detachment boarded the French transport Dives to make an escorted crossing to the Lebanon. The first problem faced by the legionnaires on landing at the port — which was teaming with journalists — was the presence of Israeli troops. The Israeli forces had prevented the port area from being secured as planned by local Lebanese troops. After a strong protest, delivered by France's Ambassador to the Lebanon, the Israelis moved off and the legionnaires were able to take up their positions.

Below: Home at last; legionnaires reach French soil for some well-deserved R&R after their Beirut mission. Opposite: This Legion officer was wounded during the peacekeeping tour.

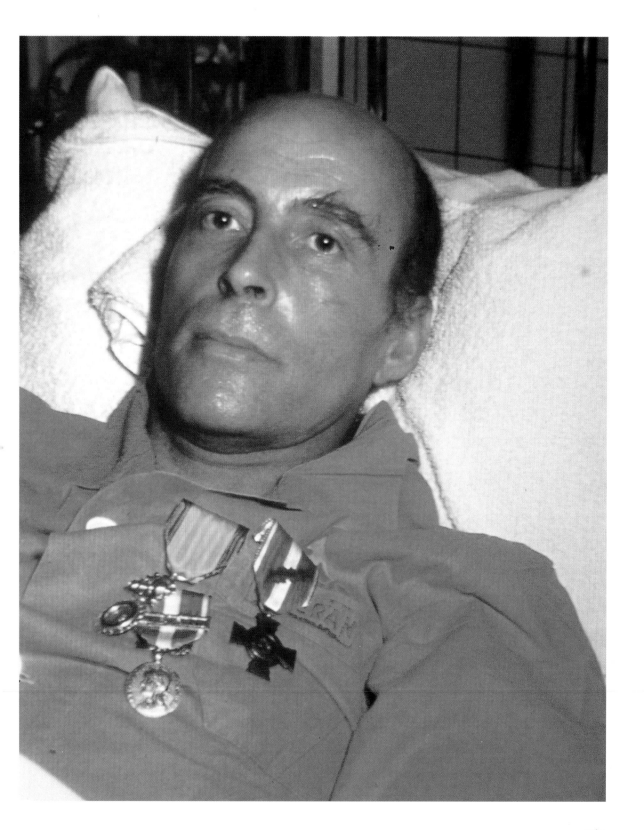

Within 30 minutes of landing, the men of 2 REP had the situation under control. Before long the Legion paras had established contact with the PLO and, after an unexpected brush with Syrian forces, both escorts and evacuees arrived at the port. Amid small arms fire and the chanting of political slogans the first PLO party to withdraw celebrated their 'success' before the television cameras of the world's press. As the men from 2 REP kept guard, the PLO embarked on the Greek-registered evacuation vessel.

The Legion's first visit to the Lebanon was a remarkable success

Their first task completed, the Legion paras secured the area for the reinforcing French troops due to arrive. Over the next few days both equipment and other units from the French Army arrived in the war-torn city. The evacuation continued and on 20 August the final party, including Arafat, arrived at the docks. Amid almost hysterical cheer-

ing the PLO leader reviewed his supporters and took the salute.

He was surrounded, at his own request and for his personal protection, by the senior officers of all the armies involved in the Lebanon peacekeeping operation. Among them was Colonel Janvier, then commanding officer of 2 REP and later to command the Task Force to Gabon in Operation Requin. Shortly afterwards, Arafat boarded the *Atlantis,* another Greek ship, which then pushed off under the protection of both French and American naval vessels.

The Legion's first visit to the Lebanon was a remarkable success. In just 12 days they had facilitated the evacuation of 9000 PLO members and their families, and the withdrawal of almost 5000 foreign troops. The Legion paras and other French airborne forces remained in the

The paras of 2 REP play an increasingly important part in the fight against terrorism. This 10-man unit is trained and equipped for hostage-rescue missions.

Lebanon until after the election of Bechir Gemayel as President of the Lebanese government, when the final elements of 2 REP were withdrawn to the aircraft carrier Foche while their vehicles were loaded aboard Dives and L'Orage.

AMX-10 RC armoured cars of 1 REC undertook mobile security patrols

The removal of French peacekeeping forces from Beirut only heralded a deterioration in the state of affairs in the Lebanon. The day after his election, 14 September 1982, President Gemayel was assassinated. On the following day the political temperature rose even further with the occupation of West Beirut by Israeli troops, and on 17 and 18 September the civilian Palestinian inhabitants of the refugee camps at Sabra and Chatila were massacred. Arafat called on the French government to stop the bloodshed and protect the Palestinians remaining in Beirut. Together with the USA, Britain and Italy, France responded as part of a multinational peacekeeping force,

An anti-terrorist training exercise at 2 REP headquarters at Calvi in Corsica. These two paras abseil down the side of the building before bursting in through the windows.

which arrived in Beirut in May 1983. The French brigade, which included elements of 1 REC and 2 REI, landed and deployed to West Beirut.

The Legion's role was, as usual, diverse. The AMX-10 RC armoured cars of 1 REC undertook mobile security patrols of the city, often engaged by the various factions who 'mistook' their vehicles for those of the 'opposition'. Of 2 REI sub-units, *5e Cie* took over the security of the French Embassy from its base among the shell-holed and bullet-ridden hotels on the once tranquil beach; *6e Cie* took up positions near the camps of Sabra and Chatila; while *7e Cie* began training Lebanese troops at a commando centre they set up in the mountains overlooking the city.

The *7e Cie* instructed the Lebanese *2e Bataillon* on how to conduct airmobile operations as part of a Franco/Lebanese agreement that the French presence

should not be seen as solely to benefit the Palestinians. The CEA (Reconnaissance and Support Company) moved into positions in southern Beirut, from which it could maintain surveillance on the airport.

These peacekeeping tasks were not without their hazards and five 2 REI legionnaires died during this, the second of the Legion's Lebanese operations. However, their casualties were light, especially when compared to those sustained by the US Marines, who lost more than 200 men in a car-bomb attack, and France's (non-Legion) paras. At the end of September 1983, the Legion were once again withdrawn from the Lebanon and were replaced by units of *11e Division Parachutiste*.

The Legion today continues to provide the French government with the spearhead of its rapid deployment force, the *Force d'Action Rapide*. The changing world and the lessening threat to European territorial security

have not diminished the need for land forces such as the FAR, and it seems highly unlikely that the Legion itself will suffer from the manpower cuts presently hitting most world armies. And in October 1990, following Iraq's invasion of Kuwait, the Legion was once again deployed, this time to Saudi Arabia as part of the multinational force in the Gulf.

'The Legion remains an invaluable asset in France's armoury'

Without doubt, the Legion has fought tougher battles in the political arena in the past and has come through them intact, as the Legion's Commandant General explained in 1990: 'The loss of French overseas territories such as Indochina and Algeria affected not only the Legion, but the French Army as a whole. But the Legion has consistently proved [itself] capable of fighting conventional as well as "colonial" wars. When France asked itself during the 1960s and the 1970s whether it still needed its *Légion Etrangère*, France was reminded of its achievements during the two world wars, and the Legion remained intact.'

Opposite: After abseiling down the side of the building, this para bursts through the window to take the terrorists by surprise. Below: A 2 REP hostage rescue exercise takes place in the officers' mess at Calvi.

So much for the reasons for the Legion's continued existence. But what role will it play now that the threat from the East has reduced so dramatically? Again the Legion's senior commander, General Le Corre, put forward his view:

The Legion is in the forefront of France's efforts to combat terrorism

'In the "post-colonial, post-cold war epoch" the need for the French Foreign Legion remains as strong as ever. Despite détente and the apparent closing of the gap between East and West, the situation can be interpreted as being more unstable than at any time over the past two decades. In this sense the Legion remains an invaluable asset in France's armoury. In addition there are many other, more recent threats. Constant change in the Muslim world, and the increase of militarism among many third world nations, has meant an increased threat level in this quarter. The Legion's unique experience in out-of-area operations has maintained its value, rather than decreased it.' Events in the Gulf in 1990 have shown how pertinent these observations are.

Closer to home, the Legion fulfils an important role in the fight against international terrorism. The democracies of Western Europe have become a target for terrorist organisation such as the Irish Republican Army, the Basque separatist movement ETA and Italy's Red Brigades. To counter this threat, governments have been forced to introduce counter-terrorist elements into their police and armed forces.

The Legion is in the forefront of France's efforts to combat terrorism, and the men of 2 REP undergo advanced counter-terrorist courses. The regiment has the expertise within its ranks to deal with any situation which

Below: In the operations room at Aubagne the Legion keeps track of its worldwide deployments. Opposite: Legionnaires prepare to disembark with a 120mm Brandt rifled mortar.

may arise. For example, when assaults on terrorist-held buildings are called, for the techniques of the 2nd company, which specialises in mountain warfare, can be utilised. In addition, the regiment conducts simulated, but highly realistic, hostage crises to prepare the men for the rescue of civilians from terrorists — exercises which often use the officer's mess in 2 REP's barracks at Calvi.

The spirit of the Legion is, essentially, the men themselves

The regiment's para-commandos have mastered all the skills of parachuting, amphibious and mountain warfare. These men are probably the most highly-trained anti-terrorist personnel available to the French government.

However, it is not the Generals or the senior French officers who make the Legion, but rather the legionnaires and their *sous-offs*. The spirit of the Legion is, essentially, the men themselves. Most modern armies, just like their predecessors, maintain that they are run by their NCOs. The Legion must surely be the foremost example of this phenomenon. For unlike most Western armies, the officers and the men are drawn from two distinct classes. The Legion recruits its officers from those who graduate top of their class at St.Cyr; the *sous-officiers* come from the ranks of legionnaires, and the legionnaires come from anywhere and everywhere. They include a good proportion of former professional servicemen, some who have been commissioned in their respective armed forces, and a large number of ex-conscript soldiers. Many of the ex-regular soldiers are more experienced than their officers but, because their non-commissioned Legion superiors have either had similar previous military service, or have spent years with the Legion, they are led by men with more experience than themselves.

Colour and ethnic background rarely enter the equation

There is a considerable amount of mutual respect between the vast majority of legionnaires and *sous-officiers*. They share much in common in terms of experience. Regardless of their past lives prior to joining the Legion, once they are a part of it they have had to undergo the same training, endure the same hardships and suffer the same privations. Colour and ethnic background rarely enter the equation, and racial tension between groups is almost entirely unknown; a man is a legion-naire, regardless of his origins. Of course some men make better soldiers than others, and the 'Brits' and Germans come high on the list, but whereas the United Kingdom's element have been said to make 'both the best and the worst legionnaires' those of German origin have the reputation of becoming the best *sous-officiers*.

'Most Brits leave because they don't fit into the system and cannot adapt to the French way of doing things', explained a Scandinavian corporal in 4 RE, who said he knew of six 'Brits' who had 'escaped' during the previous 18 months. Of this total two had deserted from 2 REP and a further two from Castelnaudary. On the other hand, the Germans adapt more readily and traditionally and comprise a large proportion of non-commissioned officers. 'I believe that in the 1970s over 50% of our *sous-offs* were German', said one commandant.

The French are generally regarded as being very different

What tension there is between different races, cultures and countries tends to come out when the legionnaires are off-duty. The various nationalities usually, but by no means always, spend their free time together with their own countrymen, in small close-knit groups. However, while the majority of such a group may be from one country it is unusual not to have at least some mix of nationalities.

For instance, someone watching a drinking-session in the legionnaires' foyer at 6 REG might notice a group regularly drinking together consisting of two 'Brits', an Irishman, a Dane and a Frenchman. The Scandinavians, and to some extent the Germans, traditionally mix well with the British, partly due to the ability of many of them to speak the English language, and perhaps also because they tend to share a similar phlegmatic outlook on life. The French on the other hand are generally regarded as being very different.

But national identity can be important to some legionnaires, especially as a means of preserving some individuality beyond the reach of the Legion and which forms some link with their past lives. 'I am a Brit', said one legionnaire in 6 REG. 'We're all proud of our nationality. OK, so we're all legionnaires but we're something else as

Opposite: Wearing life-jackets, these legionnaires listen attentively to their instructor in a class preparing them for an amphibious landing exercise.

well — we're British. In my room above my bed I've got a Union Jack. My tattoos are English, and whenever I go out of camp I wear something that shows where I come from.'

Recruiting is high and the Legion can be selective about who it accepts

This statement of extreme national loyalty comes from a young legionnaire, less than 20 years old, who before volunteering for the Legion applied to join both the Parachute Regiment and the Royal Marines. He was rejected by both because of a childhood injury, so he said, but it was obvious that the Legion had not been his first choice, and that his loyalties lay elsewhere. It is an attitude that is certainly not representative of the feelings of most legionnaires.

The traditional bond between the legionnaires themselves remains as strong as ever. Recruiting is high and the Legion can be especially selective about the volunteers it accepts. Men still join the Legion for all the old reasons. These range from 'I saw it in the fucking papers didn'a?' as reported by one Glaswegian legionnaire, to 'I had a small problem with the Politzei', the reflection of a German corporal.

The Legion's need for specialists has increased dramatically

However, things are changing, and 10 years ago few if any volunteers would have joined because they 'saw it as a good way of learning a skilled trade', which was the reason one British sergeant gave for enlisting. As warfare becomes more technical and sophisticated, the Legion's need for specialists in certain areas has increased dramatically. In fields such as computer operations and programming the British and those who speak English have a huge advantage over others, since they know the international language of the computer. Similarly, those volunteers with some technical education have a better chance of being selected, assuming they have they right attitude and physical fitness.

As the Legion moves into the computer age, is it in danger of losing some of the mystique it has acquired in the 160 years of its existence? Definitely not, according to one Legion sergeant, who comes originally from north London. Having attended two French military technical schools to learn his trade as a computer programmer, the former bank employee explains, 'quite simply people don't believe me. When I go on leave and people I know at home ask me what I do in the Legion and I tell them, they think I'm kidding. But if I tell them I work in a secret underground command centre, which explains why I don't have a "south of France suntan"' [he actually works in an office], they believe it.'

In fact, there are far more specialisations in the Legion than most people realise. They include mechanic, electrical engineer, assault pioneer, clerk, administrator, caterer, musician and technicians of all types. Among the Legion's ranks in the past have been architects, builders, carpenters — the men responsible for the construction of substantial barracks throughout the world. Sidi-bel-Abbès, for instance, was planned, designed and built almost entirely by legionnaires. Even today the Legion makes good use of its legionnaires' previously-acquired skills, and will do its utmost to further the education of any man who shows promise in a particular area.

But the Foreign Legion is still entirely infantry based, and all men, regardless of their future specialisation, undergo the same rigorous training programme. On completion they are classed as trained infantrymen and, with the exception of certain volunteers for *musique,* the Legion's marching band, all men go on to receive further practical infantry training. Such additional training almost always takes place overseas, often in an operational area such as Chad or Djibouti, and for those who wish to continue in the 00/01 skills (infantry: motorised or foot/armoured or mechanised) there is the chance to attend a commando course.

Their loyalty is of the professional soldier rather than the patriot

France's *Légion Etrangère* offers its volunteers 'the chance to fight', according to the latest Legion recruiting brochure. If the French need combat troops to do battle then they will, without doubt, call on the Legion to provide them. With the chance to fight goes the risk of injury or death. Most legionnaires are men prepared to take the risk, accepting that danger goes with the job. But they do this for the Legion, their Legion, rather than for France. Their loyalty is that of the professional soldier rather than the patriot, a fact accepted in private, if not in public, by their officers.

France provides the legionnaire with the opportunity to ply his trade of soldier. According to the Legion

Commandant General in 1990, there was a good chance of the legionnaire seeing combat at some point in his five-year contract, given the role the Legion has assumed: 'France is in a special position. It is now responsible for aiding in the defence, and enhancing the territorial security of many of its former colonies. These independent, emerging nations are reliant on France for their protection, and their security, or at least a major portion of it, depends on the ability of the Legion.'

He firmly believes that the Legion is an excellent school for a man

France needs the Legion and its fighting prowess, whether to conduct international peacekeeping duties such as in the Lebanon, release hostages as in Djibouti, or maintain the status quo, as in former territories such as Chad, Gabon and the Ivory Coast. But just what does it provide the individual legionnaire? Certainly the Legion provides a challenge for the adventurer, anonymity for the fugitive, bolt-hole for the hunted husband and family for the lonely soldier.

The spirit of the Legion burns as brightly now as it has ever done, fuelled by a fierce pride in their tradition and an equally firece desire to remain an elite fighting force.

But is that all the *Légion Etrangère* has to offer the volunteer? Perhaps the best answer to that question comes from the most experienced serving legionnaire, who in 1990 was a German who had joined the Legion as long ago as 1951.

This *sous-off,* Major Roos, confirmed in a conversation with the author that he joined the Legion at the age of 18 years when he was, as he puts it 'something of a delinquent.' He firmly believes that the Legion is an excellent school for a man, that it had certainly given him the self-confidence he needed and that above all it had allowed him 'to live the life of a man.'

Now this experienced legionnaire, a veteran of Indochina, Algeria and more besides, is nearing the end of his military career. Major Roos concludes: 'I am a contented man, proud of my achievements and at ease with my past.' Many another legionnaire, both past and present, has shared his sentiments.

ORDER OF BATTLE OF THE

OVERSEAS COMMANDS

Latin American Region:
3 REI (Guyane).

Indian Ocean Region:
Detachement de la Légion Etrangère de Mayotte (Mayotte).

Eastern Pacific Region:
5 REI (Mururou, Tahiti).

East African Region:
13 DBLE (Djibouti).

CURRENT UNITS OF THE FOREIGN LEGION

FIRST FOREIGN REGIMENT:

1 RE (1er Régiment Etranger)

Location: Aubagne, France.

Organisation: four companies:
a) headquarters company, CCSR (compagnie de commandement et des services regimentaire).
b) administrative and support company for the Legion, CSLE (compagnie des services de la Légion Etrangère).
c) personnel company for the Legion, CAPLE (compagnie administrative des personnels de la Légion Etrangère).
d) transport company, CTLE (compagnie de transit de la Légion Etrangère).
In addition, the regiment has an administrative section attached to the Ministry of Defence in Paris, three sections of the Moral Department, two information offices and fifteen recruiting offices.

FOURTH FOREIGN REGIMENT:

4 RE (4e Régiment Etranger)

Location: Castelnaudary, France.

Organisation: One headquarters company.
One NCO training company.
One specialist training company (medics, mechanics, techncians and signals).
Three new recruit training companies, each divided into four training sections.

FIFTH FOREIGN INFANTRY REGIMENT:

5 REI (5e Régiment Etranger d'Infanterie)

Location: Mururou and Tahiti.

Organisation: One headquarters company.
One sapper company.
One engineer company.
One rifle company.

SECOND FOREIGN INFANTRY REGIMENT:

2 REI (2e Régiment Etranger d'Infanterie)

Location: Nimes, France.
Organisation: One headquarters squadron.
Four rifle companies. Two scout and support companies.

THIRD FOREIGN INFANTRY REGIMENT:

3 REI (3e Régiment Etranger d'Infanterie)
Location: Guyana.

Organisation: One headquarters squadron.
Two rifle companies.
One reconnaissance and support company.

FRENCH FOREIGN LEGION

THIRTEENTH FOREIGN LEGION HALF-BRIGADE:

13 DBLE (13e Demi-brigade de la Légion Etrangère)

Location: Djibouti.

Organisation: One headquarters and support company.
One rifle company.
One armoured reconnaissance squadron.
One engineer squadron.

FIRST FOREIGN CAVALRY REGIMENT:

1 REC (1er Régiment Etranger de Cavalerie)

Location: Orange, France.

Organisation: One headquarters company.
Three armoured reconnaissance squadrons.
One anti-tank squadron.

FOREIGN LEGION DETACHMENT OF MAYOTTE:

DLEM (Detachement de Légion Etrangère de Mayotte)
The DLEM, formerly a company of 3 REI, is based on the island of Mayotte.

SIXTH FOREIGN ENGINEERING REGIMENT:

6 REG (6e Régiment Etranger de Génie)

Location: L'Ardoise, France.

Organisation: One headquarters company.
One support company.
Three combat engineer companies.

SECOND FOREIGN PARACHUTE REGIMENT:

2 REP (2e Régiment Etranger de Parachutistes)

Location: Calvi, Corsica.

Organisation: One headquarters company.
One reconnaissance and support company.
Four combat companies.

Men of 1 REC digging in with an AML-90 armoured car. The AML is armed with a 90mm cannon and a 7.62mm machine gun. It has a maximum speed of 90km/hr.

BATTLES AND CAMPAIGNS

Dates	Theatre	Units involved
1831-35	**Algeria**	Old Legion
	Campaign against the Emir of Mascara, Abd-el-Kader	
1832	Battle of Maison-Carrée	
1832	Battle of Sidi-Chabal	
1835	Battle of Mouley-Ishmael	
1835	Battle of Macta	
	(Legion dead in campaign-844)	
1835-39	**Spain**	Old Legion
	Campaign against the Carlist army	
1836	Battle of Tirapegui	
1836	Battle of Zubiri	
1837	Battle of Huesca	
	Heavy defeat for the Legion	
1837	Battle of Barbasto	
	(Legion dead in campaign — 1103)	
1836-49	**Algeria**	New Legion
1837	Battle of Djebel Dreuth	
1837	Assault on Constantine	
1839	Battle of Djidjelli	
1839	Battle of Col de Tizi	
1840, 12 May 14 June	Battles at Col de Mouzaia	
1843	Sidi-bel-Abbès becomes headquarters of 1 RE	1 RE
1844	Battle of M'Chounech	2 RE
1849 May to September	Operations in the oasis of Zaatcha	
1854-55	**Crimea**	1 RE, 2 RE
	France, Britain and Turkey against Russia	
1854	Battle of Alma 1 RE, 2 RE	
1854	Battle of Inkerman 1 RE	
1854-55	Siege of Sebastopol, 1 RE's commander, Colonel Viénot is killed in the action	
	(Legion dead in campaign — 444)	
1857	**Algeria**	
	The Legion wins the Battle of Ischeriden	2 RE
1859	**Italy**	
1859, 4 June	Battle of Magenta	1 RE, 2 RE
1859 24 June	Battle of Solferino	2 RE
	(Legion dead in campaign-143)	

Dates	Theatre	Units involved
1863-67	**Mexico**	Foreign Legion Regiment
1863 30 April	Battle of Camerone	
1863 12 Sep	Battle of Cotastla	
1865 16 Jan- 8 Feb	Siege of Oajacca	
1866	Battle of Santa Isabel	
	(Legion dead in campaign — 468)	
1870-71	**Franco-Prussian War**	Foreign Legion Regiment
1870 10 Oct	Action before Orleans	
1870 9 Nov	Battle of Coulmiers	
1871 19 Jan	Battle of Montchevis	
1871 April-May.	Siege of Neuilly	
	(Legion dead in campaign — 930)	
1870-82	**Algeria**	
1870	Abd-el-Aziz leads Berber revolt against the French.	
1882	Battle of Chotti Tigri, Berbers are defeated.	
	(Legion dead in campaign — 655)	
1883-85	**Indochina**	1 RE
1883	Capture of Son-Tay	
1884	Capture of Bac-Ninh	
1884, 3 Jan-3 Mar	Siege of Tuyen-Quang	
1885	Capture of Lang-Son	
	(Legion dead in campaign — 370)	
1892-94	**Dahomey and the Sudan**	
1892 19 Sep	Battle of Dogba	
1892 4 October	Battle of Poguessa	
1892 3 Nov	Battle of Ouakon	
1892 17 Nov	Capture of Abomey	
1892 13 October	Battle of Ackpa	
	(Legion dead in campaign — 39)	
1895-1904	**Madagascar**	1 RE
1895 9 June	Battle of Maratanano	
1895, 22 August	Capture of Andriba	
1896 22 Nov	Battle of Mahatsara	
1896 20 Dec	Capture of Maroakoha	
1898	Battle of Soaserena	
	(Legion dead in campaign — 260)	

OF THE FOREIGN LEGION

Dates	Theatre	Units involved
1903-34	**North Africa**	**1 RE, 2 RE**
1903	Battle of El Moungar	
1907	France establishes protectorate in Morocco.	
1908	Battle of Menabha	
1911	Battle of Alouana	
1914	Revolt of the Riffs in Morocco led by Abd-el-Krim.	
1918	Battle of Gaouz	
1922	Battle of Scourra	**3 RE**
1926	Revolt of the Riffs in Morocco is crushed.	
1933	Battle of Djebel Sagho	**2 RE**
	(Legion dead in campaign — 2100)	
1914-18	**France**	
1914 December	Argonne	**1 RE**
1915 May	Battle of Artois	**1 RE**
1916 July	Battle of the Somme	**RMLE**
1917 August	Battle of Cumières	**RMLE**
1918 April	Battle of Hangard Wood	**RMLE**
1915-18	**The Near East**	**Reegiment de Marche**
1915 June	Gallipoli	**Algerie**
1915 December	Serbia	
1916 November	Battle of Monastir	**RMA**
	(Total dead in World War One – 4931)	
1925	**Syria**	
1925 July	Battle of Kafer	**4 REI**
1925 September	Battle of Messifre	**4 REI, 1 REC**
1925 November	Battle of Rachaya	**1 REC**
1939-45	**World War Two**	
1940	Battle for France	**11 REI, 12 REI 21, 22 & 23 RMVE**
1940	Operation at Narvik	**13 DBLE**
1941	Syria, Free French fight Vichy forces.	**6 REI 13 DBLE**
1942	Defence of Bir Hakeim	**13 DBLE**
1943	Tunisia	**1 REIM**
1944	Campaign in Italy, invasion of France.	**13 DBLE, 1 REC, RMLE**
1945	Campaign in Germany	**RMLE, 1 REC, 13 DBLE**
	(Legion dead in campaign — 9017)	

Dates	Theatre	Units involved
1947-54	**Indochina**	
1948	Battle at Phu-Tong-Hoa	**3 REI**
1949	Action at Ninh-Phuoc	**2 REI**
1950	Action around Dong-Khe	**3 REI 1 BEP**
1951	Battle at An-Hoa	**13 DBLE**
1954	Defence of Dien Bien Phu	**1 & 2 BEP 2 & 3 REI 13 DBLE, 5 REI**
	(Legion dead in campaign — 10,483)	
1954-62	**Algeria**	**1 & 2 RE, 2, 3, 4, & 5 REI,13 DBLE, 1 & 2 REC, 1 & 2 BEP, 1 REP**
1957	Battle of Algiers	
1961	Rebellion against de Gaulle, 1 REP is disbanded	**1 REP**
1962	Algerian war ends.	
	(Legion dead in campaign — 1855)	
1956	**Egypt**	**1 REP**
	Anglo-French landings at Suez	**2 REC**
1967	**Algeria**	**1 REC**
	Last Legion unit leaves the country.	
1969-70	**Chad**	**2 REP**
	Intervention to restore order. (Legion dead — 8)	
1976	**Djibouti**	**2 REP 13 DBLE**
	Rescue of schoolchildren from terrorists.	
1978	**Zaire**	**2 REP**
	Legion rescues European settlers in Kolwezi. (Legion dead — 5)	
1978-79	**Chad**	**2 REI, 2 REC**
	Second French intervention. (Legion dead — 1)	
1982-83	**Lebanon**	**2 REP 2 REI, 1 RE,1 REC**
	Legion forms part of multinational peacekeeping force in Beirut. (Legion dead — 5)	
1983-84	**Chad**	**1 REC, 2 REP**
	Third French intervention.	
1990	**Gabon**	**2 REP 2 REI**
	Deployment to safeguard French citizens.	
1990	**Djibouti**	**13 DBLE**
	French forces put on alert ready to intervene in the Gulf in support of UN sanctions against Iraq.	

WEAPONS AND EQUIPMENT OF THE FRENCH FOREIGN LEGION

Because of its out-of-area responsibilities and its role within the Rapid Action Force, the Foreign Legion uses equipment which is capable of high tactical mobility. It therefore uses wheeled armoured fighting vehicles (AFVs), helicopters and C160 Transall transport aircraft, as well as light trucks and jeeps. The weapons used by the Legion are no different to those which are used by the rest of the French Army. However, being primarily an infantry force, the Legion is mainly equipped with light weapons.

FA MAS 5.56 mm automatic rifle

This rifle is small, rugged and extremely versatile, and offers the user several options in the mode of fire and method of use. Its 'Bull Pup' layout makes it a compact weapon and therefore ideal for paratroop operations. The barrel is only slightly shorter than that of the M16 but in overall size the FA MAS is 30 mm shorter. As well as a single shot function the weapon has an option for semi- or full-automatic fire and there is a three-round-burst counter that is tucked away in the butt, just in front of the butt pad.

The sling is considered to be an integral part of the rifle and its use recommended for all firing, especially when a steady shot is required. The weapon can be easily converted for either left- or right-shoulder firing. The cheek piece is taken off and turned round, exposing an ejection opening on the opposite side. The bolt is taken out and the extractor claw and ejector are swapped from one side to the other. The operation only takes a few minutes.

A small knife-bayonet clips on to the muzzle, and the mounting accepts the standard range of French grenades. There is a short version of the rifle, called the FA MAS Commando, which is intended for use by special forces units. The barrel has been shortened to 405 mm but in all other respects it is the same as the service weapon.

The only disadvantage with this weapon is that the tall bipod and magazine height lift the rifle higher in the prone position than most other weapons which produces a high firing profile. In addition, the bipod position allows only a small arc of fire.

Length: 757mm.
Weight: 3.61kg.
Effective range: 300m.
Cyclic rate of fire: 900-1000rpm.
Practical rate of fire: 50-125
Muzzle velocity: 960m/sec.
Magazine: 25-round detachable box.

Above: Legion infantrymen in NBC suits and masks. The legionnaire in the foreground is using the LRAC anti-tank weapon, capable of penetrating 400mm of armour. Opposite: Paras of 2 REP pack up their gear after a successful landing.

F1 7.5mm Rifle

This weapon is a bolt-action rifle which is offered in three versions: Model A for sniping, Model B for competition shooting and Model C for big-game hunting. Though of conventional design it is made with a high degree of precision, with much effort being directed towards the machining of components. Butt length can be adjusted by using a series of extension pieces and a bipod can be fitted to aid steadier shooting. The rifle is usually fitted with a telescopic sight for daylight use with a night sight available for shooting in poor light.

Length: 1138mm.

Weight: 5.20kg.

Range: 300m.

Muzzle velocity: 853m/sec.

Magazine: 10-round detachable box.

Model 1952 7.5mm Light Machine Gun

This is a general-purpose light machine gun which is equipped with crutch supports, bipod, shoulder-piece and a carrying handle. When using armour-piercing ammunition the weapon is capable of penetrating 12mm of armour plating at 100 metres.

Length: 1.165m.

Weight of weapon: 9.9kg.

Weight of bipod: 2.0kg.

Effective range: 600m (bipod), 1000m (tripod).

Cyclic rate of fire: 700rpm.

Above: The VAB armoured personnel carrier is fully amphibious. Opposite: Firing the HOT — the High- subsonic, Optical remote-guided, Tube-fired anti-tank missile.

81mm Mortar

Barrel length: 1.15m.

Weight: 29.4kg.

Elevation: 30/85 degrees.

Sustained rate of fire: 15rpm.

Maximum rate of fire: 25rpm.

Maximum range: 4.1km.

Shell weight: 3.3kg.

20mm Machine Cannon M621

This is an automatic weapon with an electrical firing mechanism which was designed for use on light transports.

Length: 2207mm.

Weight: 58kg.

Rate of fire: 300 or 740rpm.

LRAC F1 89mm Light Anti-Tank Weapon

This weapon is usually operated by a team of two, the gunner and a loader. It is capable of piercing 400mm of armour plating or 1000m of concrete.

Length: 1600mm (when firing).
Weight: 5.5kg.
Weight of rocket: 2.2kg.
Effective range: 400m.

MILAN Anti-Tank Weapon

The MILAN is a two/three man medium anti-tank missile system which is in use in at least 30 countries. Usually fired from the ground with the firer prone it can also be fitted to various types of vehicle. After firing, the missile is kept on target by wire-guided remote control, operated by keeping the infra-red sight on the target throughout its flight.

Missile length: 769mm.
Fin span: 265mm.
Weight (with launching block and tripod): 17kg.
Minimum range: 25-280m.
Maximum range: 2km.
Flight speed: 200m/sec.
Armour penetration: 350-500mm.

HOT Anti-Tank Guided Missile

The High-subsonic, Optical remote-guided, Tube-fired anti-tank missile is usually fitted to helicopters, however it can also be fired from vehicles and surface positions. Like MILAN it uses the SACLOS (semi-automatic command to line of sight) guidance system.

Missile length: 1275mm.
Missile diameter: 130mm.
Minimum range: 75m.
Maximum range: 4km.
Flight speed: 250m/sec.
Armour penetration: 800mm.

TRANSALL C-130

The Transall transport aircraft provides French paratroop forces, including 2 REP, with the means to move large amounts of men quickly to a landing zone. The aerial refuelling probe has given the Transall increased range, which has resulted in its becoming a limited strategic transport aircraft.

Maximum speed, at 4875m: 513km/hr.
at sea level: 177km/hr.
Service ceiling: 8230m.
Maximum range, with 8000kg payload: 5095km.
with 16,000kg payload: 1853km.
Maximum payload: 16,000kg.
Troops carried: 93.

Powerplant: Two Rolls-Royce Mk22 turboprops.
Internal fuel load: 22,440kg.

SUPER FRELON SA 321

France has around 17 of these helicopters remaining in service, divided between two squadrons. Virtually all French Super Frelons have received the nose-mounted ORB-31D radar to allow them to launch Exocet missiles.

Cruising speed at sea level: 248km/hr.
Service ceiling: 3100m.
Maximum range with 3500kg payload: 1020km.
Patrol endurance: 4 hours.
Initial climb rate: 300m per minute.
Troops carried: 30.
Powerplant: Three Turbomeca Turmo III C7 turboshafts.

PUMA SA30

There are some 145 Puma helicopters in French service, most are operated by army aviation but some 40 aircraft serve with the air force and trial units. Some 40 % of the French Puma force have plastic main rotor blades. The crew consists of one or two pilots plus a loadmaster.

Cruising speed: 262km/hr.
Service ceiling: 4600m.
Maximum range: 618m.
Endurance: 3 hours 20 minutes.
Troops carried: 16.
Powerplant: Turbomeca Makila IA1 turbo shafts.

VAB armoured personnel carrier

The VAB (*Véhicule de l'Avant Blindée*, or front armoured vehicle) is produced in 4 by 4 and 6 by 6 configurations. It has an all-welded hull with the driver and commander at the front. The VAB is fully amphibious and French Army vehicles are equipped with NBC systems and passive night-vision equipment.

Crew: Two.
Troops carried: 10.
Powerplant: One MAN diesel engine.
Maximum speed: 92km/hr.
Maximum range: 1000km.

FL 501 Light Vehicle

The FL 501 is a light airportable vehicle designed for the use of airborne troops. One C-160 Transall can carry six FL 501s ready for air dropping or 12 ready for delivery as cargo.

Crew: One.
Maximum load: 500kg.
Maximum speed: 80km/hr.
Road range: 200km.
Fuel capacity: 25 litres.
Fording: 0.4 metres.

Hotchkiss M 201 400kg Light Vehicle

The basic vehicle is used as a radio/command vehicle by the French Army. The layout is conventional with the engine at the front and a cargo area at the rear, the windscreen can be folded down on to the top of the bonnet.

Crew: One.
Passengers: Three.
Maximum load: 400kg.
Maximum speed: 100km/hr.
Range: 348km.
Fuel capacity: 49 litres.
Fording: 0.533 metres.

AMX-10 armoured reconnaissance vehicle

Used by 1 REC, this vehicle is heavily armed and can be used for a number of roles. It is a six-wheeled diesel-powered vehicle constructed of aluminium and is fully amphibious with an overpressure NBC defence system.

Crew: Four.
Maximum speed: 85km/hr.
Range: 800km.
Main gun: 105mm.
Co-axial: 7.62mm.
Armour: 40mm.

Above (top): A Milan missile launcher, mounted on a Hotchkiss jeep, just after the missile has been fired — hence the empty tube. Above: A legionnaire takes aim with the F1 sniper's rifle.

THE RANKS OF THE LEGION

Listed below is a table of French ranks with their British and American equivalents. In the French army several ranks come under one term; *soldat (legionnaire) de 2e classe* up to *caporal-chef* are *hommes du rang*; *sergent* up to *major* are *sous-officiers*; *aspirant* up to *capitaine* are *officiers subalternes*; and *commandant* up to *colonel* are *officiers superieurs*.

AMERICAN RANKS	FRENCH RANKS	BRITISH RANKS
General of the Army	Maréchal de France	Field Marshal
General	Général d'Armée	General
Lieutenant-General	General de Corps d'Armée	Lieutenant-General
Major-General	Général de Division	Major-General
Brigadier-General	Général de Brigade	Brigadier
Colonel	Colonel	Colonel
Lieutenant-Colonel	Lieutenant-colonel	Lieutenant Colonel
Major	Commandant	Major
Captain	Capitaine	Captain
First Lieutenant	Lieutenant	Lieutenant
Second Lieutenant	Sous-lieutenant	Second Lieutenant
-	Aspirant	-
-	Major	-
Chief Warrant Officr	Adjudant-chef	Warrant Officer I
Warrant Officer Junior Grade	Adjudant	Warrant Officer II
First Sergeant	Sergent-major (obsolete)	-
Master Sergeant	Sergent-chef	Staff Sergeant
Sergeant First Class	-	
Sergeant	Sergent (1)	Sergeant
-	Caporal-chef	-
Corporal	Caporal (2)	Corporal
Private First Class	Soldat (legionnaire) de 1re classe	Lance Corporal
Private	Soldat (legionnaire) de 2e classe	Private

NOTES
1) In the French cavalry *Maréchal des logis* is used instead of *Sergent*.
2) In the French artillery *brigadier* is used instead of *Caporal*.

GLOSSARY OF TERMS AND ABBREVIATIONS

A moi la Legion – 'To me the Legion'. The legionnaire's traditional cry for help. The Legion was often unpopular with both French and native levies and so the custom arose of raising this cry to fellow legionnaires in times of distress.

ALN – Armee de Liberation Nationale: Algerian National Liberation Army, the military wing of the FLN.

Appel – roll call.

Battalion – A unit composed of between 500 and 800 legionnaires. For example, the Legion battalions which were sent to the Far East in the 1880's averaged around 600 men each.

Bataillon de marche – An elite unit made up of experienced legionnaires.

BEP – Bataillon Etrangère de Parachutistes: Foreign parachute battalion.

Bled – French military term for the outback.

BMC – Bordel Militaire Controlé: Military brothel.

BSLE – Bureau des Statistiques de la Legion Etrangère: The Legion's records office at Aubagne.

Le Boudin - 'The Black Pudding': The marching song of the Foreign Legion. It is believed that the title alludes to the sausage-shaped tent-roll which was carried on top of a legionnaire's back-pack.

Cafard – A mythical black beetle which the legionnaires believed invaded the body and gnawed the brain, resulting in madness.

Camerone – The name of a small hamlet in Mexico, on 30 April 1863 the site of an epic battle between a company of Legionnaires under the command of Capitaine Danjou and an army of 2000 Mexicans. The battle is commemorated each year at every Legion station. At Aubagne the wooden hand of Capitaine Danjou is paraded and carried to the Monument to the Dead.

CCS – Compagnie de Commandement et des Services: Headquarters company.

CEA – Compagnie d'Eclairage et Appui: Reconnaissance and Support Company.

Colon – European settler.

Corvee – Fatigue duties awarded to junior ranks.

Company – Unit made up of between 100 and 230 legionnaires.

DBLE – Demi-Brigade de la Légion Etrangère: Foreign Legion Half Brigade.

EVs – Engagés Volontaires: Legion recruits.

FAR – Force d'Action Rapide: Rapid Action Force.

Fellagha – Arab guerrilla.

FLN – Front de Liberation Nationale: National Liberation Front. Political organisation formed in Algeria in 1954 to bring about the end of French rule and the creation of an independent Algeria.

Foyer – A regiment's mess.

GLE – Groupement de Legion Etrangère: Foreign Legion Group.

IILE – Invalide Institution de la Legion Etrangère: The Legion's retirement home at Puyloubier.

Jihad – Holy War.

Katiba – FLN company.

Képi Blanc – White Kepi. This piece of headgear has become the symbol of the Legion. Sous-Officiers wear a dark blue kepi.

Legio Patria Nostra – The legion is our homeland: The motto of the Legion.

Magrheb - 'Land of the setting sun'. The countries of Tunisia, Algeria and Morocco.

Monument aux Morts – Monument to the Dead. The Legion's war memorial, originally built at Sidi-bel-Abbès and dedicated on 30 April 1931, the one hundredth anniversary of the Legion. After the Algerian war it was transported to France and re-erected at the Quartier Viénot, Aubagne.

NCO – Noncommissioned officer.

OAS – Organisation de l'Armee Secrete: Secret Army Organisation. Terrorist organisation formed in January 1961 by French officers. Its aim was to use violence to ensure that Algeria remained under French control.

Paquetage – A legionnaire's clothing kit.

Pied Noir – Black Foot: A European settler in Algeria.

Quartier Capitaine Danjou – The headquarters of 4 REI at Castelnaudary.

Quartier Vienot – The headquarters of 1 RE at Aubagne.

RE – Régiment Etranger:Foreign Regiment.

REC – Régiment Etranger de Cavalrie: Foreign Cavalry Regiment. After the formation of 1 REC in 1921 all other regiments had to include the designation 'infantry' in their titles.

Opposite: Camp Raffalli, at Calvi in Corsica, is home to the Foreign Legion's only parachute regiment, 2 REP. As part of the Rapid Action Force, 2 REP are on permanent standby.

Rectification d'etat civile – Certification that the name adopted by a legionnaire in the Legion is his true name. New recruits can, if they choose, be issued with a new name, nationality and date of birth by the Legion. After three years a legionnaire can revert to his own name or be issued with another false one.

REG – Regiment Etranger de Genie: Foreign Engineering Regiment.

Regiment – Army unit composed of around four battalions.

Regiment de marche – Unit composed of experienced legionnaires assembled for a specific task.

REI – Regiment Etranger d'Infanterie: Foreign Infantry Regiment.

REP – Regiment Etranger de Parachutistes: Foreign Parachute Regiment.

Riff – An inhabitant of the Atlas mountains of Morocco.

RMLE – Regiment de Marche de la Légion Etrangère: Foreign Legion Marching Regiment.

RMLE-EOP – Regiment de Marche de la Légion Etrangère-Extrème Orient: Foreign Legion Marching Regiment – Far East.

RMVE – Regiment de Marche de Volontaires Etrangères: Marching Regiment of Foreign Volonteers.

Sidi-bel-Addès – The headquarters of the Legion when it was based in Algeria. It had been a permanent Legion camp since 1840.

SNCO – Senior noncommissioned officer.

Tenue de combat – Combat kit.

Wilaya – Military district.

PICTURE ACKNOWLEDGEMENTS

1) Robin Adshead 155, 156, 157.
2) E.C.P.A. 90, 91, 94, 95, 97, 99, 106, 107, 109, 111.
3) I.W.M. 122.
4) P. MacDonald 10, 12, 13, 14, 21, 28, 33, 35, 36, 40, 42, 49B, 50, 51, 52, 53, 56, 57, 58T, 58B, 64, 73, 74, 85, 86, 92, 93, 130, 165, 172, 175.
5) Brown Packaging 152T/L, 152T/R, 153, 154.
6) Rex Features 16, 24, 27, 34, 55, 62, 77, 80, 117, 123, 125, 131, 162, 166T, 170, 171, 173, 177.
7) Jim Short 19, 148, 149, 150, 151.
8) F. Spooner Pictures Cover, title page, 6, 8, 11, 18, 22, 23, 29, 30, 31, 32, 35, 39, 44, 45, 49T, 54, 60, 63, 65, 66, 67, 68, 69, 71, 72, 75, 76, 78, 79, 83, 85, 96, 118, 127, 128, 129, 133, 146, 158, 159, 160, 167, 168, 169, 174, 179.
9) Henri Beureau / Sygma 135, 136, 138, 139, 140, 141, 143T, 143B, 144, 145.

BIBLIOGRAPHY

Anderson, Roy, *Devils, Not Men,* David & Charles, 1987

Bergot, Erwan, *The French Foreign Legion,* Allan Wingate Ltd., 1975

Elford, George Robert, *Devil's Guard,* New English Library, 1972

Geraghty, Tony, *March Or Die,* Fontana, 1987

Horne, Alistair, *A Savage War Of Peace, Algeria 1954-62,* Macmillan London Ltd., 1977

Jennings, Christian, *Mouthful Of Rocks,* Bloomsbury, 1989

McLeave, Hugh, *The Damned Die Hard,* Saxon House, 1974

Murray, Simon, *Legionnaire,* Sidgwick & Jackson, 1978

O'Ballance, Edgar, *The Story Of The French Foreign Legion,* Purnell Book Services Ltd., 1961

Sergent, Pierre, *La Légion,* 1985

Thomas, Nigel, *The French Foreign Legion,* Sentinel, 1973

Windrow, Martin, and *Braby, Wayne, French Foreign Legion Paratroops,* Osprey Publishing Ltd., 1985

Young, John Robert, *The French Foreign Legion,* Thames & Hudson, 1970

LE BOUDIN — MARCHING SONG OF THE LEGION

Tiens, voilà du boudin, voilà du boudin, voilà du boudin
Pour les Alsaciens, les Suisses et les Lorrains,
Pour les Belges, il n'y en a plus, pour les Belges il n'y en a plus,
Ce sont des tireurs au cul.
Pour les Belges il n'y en a plus, pour les Belges il n'y en a plus,
Ce sont des tireurs au cul.

Nous sommes des dégourdis, nous sommes des lascars,
Des type pas ordinaires,
Nous avons souvent notre cafard,
Nous sommes des Légionnaires.

Au Tonkin, la Légion immortelle
A Tuyen Quang illustra notre drapeau.
Héros de Camerone et frères modèles
Dormez en paix en vos tombeaux.

Nos anciens ont su mourir
Pour la gloire de la Légion,
Nous saurons bien tous périr
Suivant la tradition.

Au cours de nos campagnes lointanes,
Affrontant la fièvre et le feu,
Nous oublions avec nos peines
La mort qui nous oublie si peu
Nous, la Légion.

Well, there's blood sausage, blood sausage, blood sausage,
For the Alsatians, the Swiss and the Lorrainers,
For the Belgians there's none left,
For the Belgians there's none left,
They are shirkers
For the Belgians there's none left,
For the Belgians there's none left,
They are shirkers.

We are keen and we are mean
No ordinary fellows,
We often get the blues
We are Legionnaires.

In Tonkin the immortal Legion
Brought glory to our flag at Tuyen Quang.
Heros of Camerone and model brothers
Sleep peacefully in your tombs.

Our forebears knew how to die
For the glory of the Legion,
We will all know how to perish
Following tradition.

In our distant campaigns
Faced with fever and fire
We forget, along with our troubles,
Death, who rarely forgets
Us, the Legion.